BARNDOMINIUM
FLOOR PLANS AND DESIGNS

From Blueprint to Beauty : Your Comprehensive Guide to Floor Plans and Designs

Schmid B. Milligan

Contents

Introduction

Welcome to the world of Barndominiums, where innovation meets elegance, and architectural wonders unfold. In this comprehensive guide, we embark on a journey through the realm of "Barndominium Floor Plans and Designs," a book meticulously curated to inspire and guide you in the creation of your dream home.

Unveiling the Essence of Barndominium Living

At the heart of this exploration lies the concept of Barndominium living—an architectural trend that seamlessly blends rustic charm with contemporary design. Imagine a home that echoes the tranquility of rural life while offering the modern amenities and customizable spaces that cater to your unique lifestyle. This book is your key to unlocking the potential of Barndominium living and understanding the intricate dance between form and functionality.

The Blueprint to Beauty

Our journey begins with the fundamental aspect of any dream home—the floor plan. Barndominiums are celebrated for their open and flexible layouts, and this book delves deep into the art of crafting these blueprints. From spacious living areas that encourage family gatherings to thoughtfully designed kitchens that inspire culinary creativity, each floor plan is a canvas awaiting your personal touch.

Navigating the Architectural Wonders

As we navigate through the pages, be prepared to witness architectural wonders that redefine the concept of home. Barndominiums are not just houses; they are statements of individuality and style. Discover how architects and designers have pushed the boundaries, fusing traditional barn aesthetics with modern sophistication. This exploration is a testament to the endless possibilities that Barndominium designs offer, making a bold statement in the world of residential architecture.

Decoding the Art of Living

Barndominium living is an art—an art that balances elegance with functionality. Through this book, you will delve into the core principles of designing a space that resonates with your lifestyle. From the choice of materials that enhance the rustic appeal to the strategic placement of windows that invite natural light, every detail contributes to the artistry of living in a Barndominium.

Personalizing Your Dream Home

One of the standout features of Barndominiums is their adaptability to personal preferences. This book serves as your guide to the customization process, empowering you to transform a mere blueprint into your dream home. Whether you envision a cozy retreat nestled in the countryside or a modern urban oasis, Barndominiums offer the flexibility to manifest your vision.

A Comprehensive Approach

This guide takes a comprehensive approach, covering not only the aesthetic aspects of Barndominiums but also the practical considerations. We address questions of sustainability, energy efficiency, and the seamless integration of technology, ensuring that your dream home is not only beautiful but also environmentally conscious and technologically advanced.

Your Journey Starts Here

Embark on this journey with us as we unravel the secrets of Barndominium living. Whether you are a homeowner seeking inspiration, an architect exploring innovative designs, or simply someone intrigued by the marriage of rustic charm and modern luxury, there is something for everyone within these pages.

"Barndominium Floor Plans and Designs" is more than a book—it's a guide to creating a living space that reflects your personality, values, and aspirations. It's an invitation to imagine, innovate, and ultimately craft a home where memories are made and dreams find their foundation.

Join us as we explore the enchanting world of Barndominiums, where each page brings you closer to the realization of your ideal living space. Your journey to a personalized and architecturally stunning home begins now. Welcome home!

Chapter 1

What is a Barndominium?

These days, it seems like you can't read anything about homes or home trends without also reading a book about the newest styles. You may have heard of tiny homes, van homes, and shipping container homes if you've been paid attention to the new kinds of homes that are coming out. But the word you may have found by accident and been most surprised by is probably "barndominium." You might be interested in what the name means besides just finding it interesting. A "barndominium" can make you think of a lot of different things. But what it really means and what it can do for you are even more interesting.

You can choose if a barndominium is right for you if you know what it is and how it's different from other home styles. You should be able to build any type of home and pick the right one. To do that, you should know everything there is to know about it.

What does a Barndominium really mean?

"Barndominium" is made up of the words "barn" and "condominium." It's pretty clear that barndominiums are also called "barndos" and "barn homes." No matter what they're called, the main idea stays the same. A barndominium is a house made from a new or used metal barn. Because a barndominium doesn't need the complicated wood frame and other building parts that a house does, this is very important. A post frame system holds them together. Some people say that building a house with a post frame is easier than with a regular house frame.

In a metal post frame building, the posts are driven into the ground instead of being built on top of each other and held up by them. A concrete block floor is usually put down first, and then the metal building is put on top of it. Then, the inside of the metal pole barn is put together like a house. This is why the inside of barndominiums looks like the inside of all other houses. You would never be able to tell the difference between the two from the inside of a barndominium. This is one reason why they're so well-known. Inside, you can do almost anything you want, just like in a regular house. It's simple to make them. It's easy to determine "what is a barndominium"; it's basically a house that's easier to put together.

How the Barndominium came to be

Building a house inside a barn is not a new idea. On fields, people often live in or next to their stables so they can watch over their animals at night. This helped farmers stay awake and not give up their way of life just because work was over. But the word "barndominium" was first used in a book from 1989 that was published in the New York Times. The book begins by asking, "What is a barndominium?" It then goes on to describe a horse-friendly neighborhood in Connecticut where people could live with their horses in homes that also had horse stalls. Developer Karl Nilsen came up with this idea, and the group became famous for its unique ideas and way of life.

Barndominiums didn't seem to be talked about much after this first book in The New York Times. Before an HGTV show called Fixer Upper, where the hosts changed an old barn into a modern, high-end home. This made more people want to use metal post-frame buildings, which led to more calls for builders to make these types of homes. But they're best known in the south. Since then, they've been seen all over the country. However, barndominiums can be built anywhere, and they can be useful for people who want to live in a unique house. People don't ask "What is a barndominium?" as often as they used to.

Someone who wants to build a barndominium.

A barndominium might be a good choice for most people, but some people might really enjoy living there. What about a barndominium? It might be the best choice for you if you want to make your home exactly how you want it. The inside of a barndominium can be changed in almost any way you desire. It might be a good fit for you if that sounds like something you'd be interested in. Also, because it's easier to put together, a barndominium is often less expensive. This lets the person who is building the house know a lot of options for what they can afford.

Price is something else to think about. Folks who can't normally pay for the high cost of building a custom house might like the idea of a barndominium. Most of the time, it costs a lot less to build a barndominium than a regular house. We will talk about this some more in the book that's coming up. This means that people who are having trouble finding the money to build a new home might be able to afford to build a barndominium instead. This lets people who are getting their first home or who haven't built a custom home yet get one.

How is a barndominium built?

A metal post frame building kit is often used to create a barndominium. They can also be built from scratch by people who are up for the task. Concrete slab foundations aren't the same as other types of home foundations, and they might be easier to build and set up. This is the ground that most barndominiums are built on. The main thing that sets a barndominium apart from a normal house is that it doesn't have any support beams like a house does. This means the metal pole frame can be put together much faster than a normal house. There is less money spent and more ease for both the builder and the person who orders the building.

Barndominiums can also be bought as kits that can be put together by different companies. You have everything you need to build your barndominium in these kits. If you don't want to start from scratch, this is a great option. When it's time to put it together, you can often get help from the company that made it. Barndominium kits will come with clear directions. Sometimes, the company that makes the kit will send a qualified builder to your location to put it together.

Who builds farm-style homes?

You don't have to build your barndominium by yourself if you want to. One bad thing about barndominiums for a long time was that not many people knew how to put them together. Good news: that's no longer the case. This type of building is so popular that many builders now know how to make them. Some people build them all the time. A year goes by, and new builders from all over the country who know how to build with metal poles show up. Since there are more of them, builders are not likely to ask you, "What is a barndominium?"

So, here are some things you should look for in a builder of barndominiums. When you hire someone, make sure they've worked on projects like yours before. There are a lot of different kinds of builders, and some may not know how to erect a metal pole barn. Also, look for a builder who gets along well with the people whose homes they've already done work for. Because building a house is such a personal job, you want someone to be there for you the whole time.

Is it possible to borrow money to buy a barndominium?

A lot of people used to have trouble getting loans for buildings and barndominiums. Most of the time, this was because banks didn't fully understand these types of homes and wouldn't give money for something they didn't fully understand. But that's not the same as it used to be. The number of banks that ask what a barndominium is going down because they are getting more and more popular. This is usually the case in southern states where barndominiums are popular.

If you need a bank to lend you money for a barndominium, make sure that they also lend money for farms. It is very important to do this if you plan to farm on your land. A farm bank is more likely to give you money if they think the idea will fit in with farming in the area. This could be a good place to start if you are new to building a barndominium. It's also important to know how to pay for your barndominium and what kind of protection you should get for your insurance.

What is a Barndominium Land plot?

One of the main things people want to know about barndominiums is how to find the right land for them. Finding land for your barndominium is the most important thing. There are many places online where you can look for land. There should be enough space on the land you buy in the country for you to build your house, but not so much that you can't get around. It can be pricey to add services to a lot, so it's best if the land you buy already has them.

You should also look for land that has been cleared enough for you to build on. You will need to clean up any land you find, but it won't cost a lot of money to get rid of the trees and other plants. Before you start building, make sure the land is ready. This will save you a lot of time and money in the long run.

What Kinds of Floor Plans Does a Barndominium Come With?

You can design almost any floor plan for your barndominium. Simply put, the concrete block base of a barndo should let you make any shape you can think of. A barndominium can have a porch that goes all the way around, more than one bedroom and bathroom, and a lot of other cool features. Your thoughts are the only thing stopping you. It might be easier to plan your barndominium if you use tools for plans.

Traditional and barndominium homes are the two main types.

The main difference between a barndominium and a normal house is the price. Building a house costs a lot more than building a barndominium. It's because they're very simple to set up. The first part of building a standard house can take up to a year. But if everything goes as planned, building a barndominium takes about 6 months.

Another big difference between taking care of a house and a barndominium is how you clean it. A lot of wood is used to make classic homes. Because of this, rot, mold, and mildew can grow on them. A barndominium is mostly made of metal, so it will be strong enough to withstand wind, rain, and ice.

That being said

Find out what a barndominium is and how it's different from a regular house. This will help you get your project off the ground. A barndominium has a lot of good points and almost no bad ones. Now that you know how to build one of these beautiful, one-of-a-kind homes, you can decide if it's right for you and your family.

5 Bedroom 2 Story Barndominium Floor Plans

One of the benefits of a two-story, five-bedroom house plan is definitely flexibility. Open floor designs and, of course, the charming curb appeal of a barndominium—which is very in—are features of these house plans. View these two-story, five-bedroom barndominium floor plans.

Floor Plan for a Two-Story, Five-Bedroom Barndominium

The layout of a two-story barndominium featuring five bedrooms and an exterior front

The main floor plan of a five-bedroom, two-story barndominium

The upper level layout of a five-bedroom, two-story barndominium

This traditional five-bedroom barndominium features gables, board-and-batten siding, and stone veneer accents. The front porch and entryway add elegance to this floor plan. Wide windows complement the modern open design and stunning garden vista that are shown through the entrance. The barndominium layout's two levels are filled with these incredibly beautiful windows. The ground level main suite has two walk-in closets, a full bathroom with a tub, and entrance to the back terrace. The first level also has a guest bedroom that serves as a home office.

On the second floor, there are three guest bedrooms, each featuring a spacious walk-in closet. The walkway that leads to the guest suites also offers views of the great room below.

The layout of a five-bedroom, two-story barndominium featuring an in-law suite

Floor plan for a two-story, five-bedroom barndominium featuring a front porch and an in-law suite

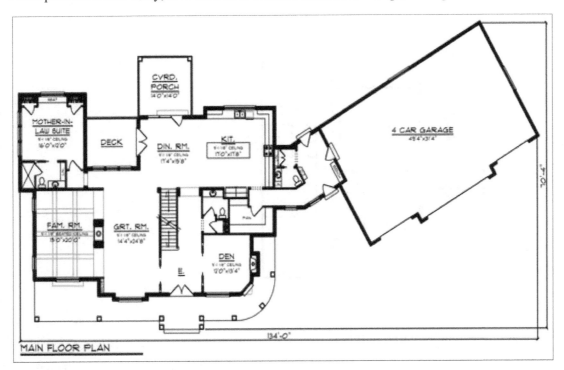

Two-story barndominium's main floor plan with five bedrooms and an in-law suite

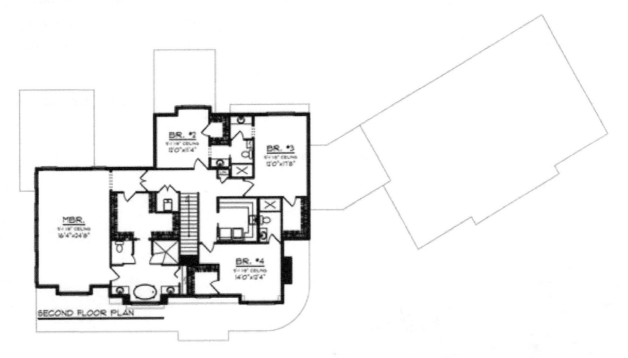

A two-story barndominium with five bedrooms and an upper-floor in-law suite is shown in the floor plan.

This two-story barndominium floor plan's versatility is further enhanced by the in-law suite located on the first level. Adjacent to the in-law suite, the formal family room features two sitting areas divided by a two-way fireplace. Having a separate in-law suite on the first floor is ideal for any relatives who may be living there. Upstairs are three guest bedrooms, all of which have walk-in closets and convenient access to the laundry area. The luxurious master suite, which is on the second floor, has an incredible walk-in closet.

Five-bedroom, two-story vintage barndominium floor plan

Five-Bedroom Traditional Two-Story Barndominium Floor Plan with Front Exterior

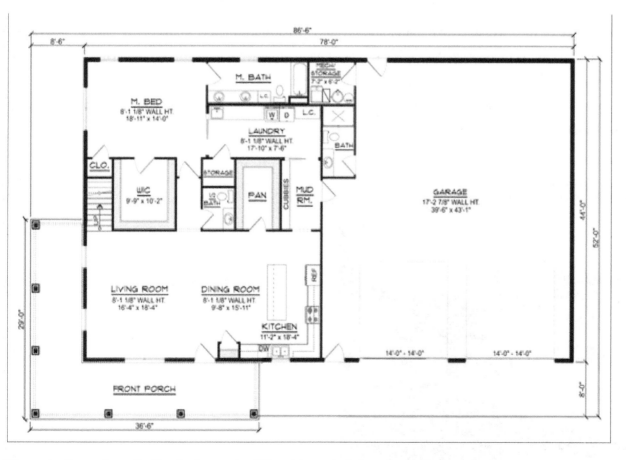

The main floor plan of a five-bedroom traditional two-story barndominium

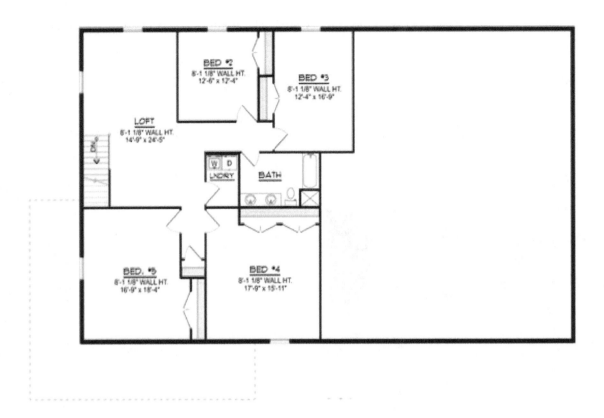

Upper Floor Plan of a Traditional Two-Story Barndominium with Five Bedrooms

The roomy two-car garage of this two-story barndominium layout is what immediately grabs our attention. The raised ceilings and workshop space in the two-car garage allow for the storage of larger vehicles and equipment. The first level features a convenient mud room that provides access to the walk-in laundry room from the garage. The laundry area is attached to the main suite, which features a walk-in closet and a private bathroom. All of the guest bedrooms, the cozy loft, and the second laundry room are located on the second floor.

Unique five-bedroom two-story barndominium

Gorgeous five-bedroom, two-story barndominium with an outside front

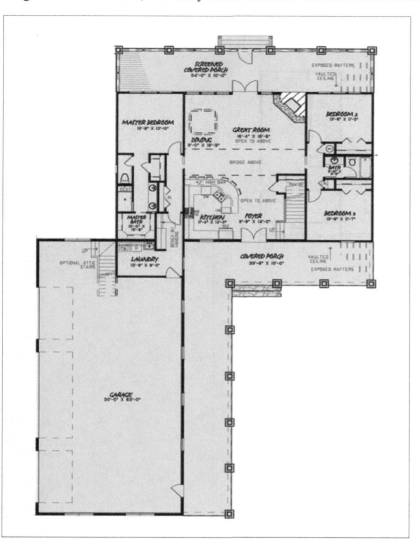

Unique Five-Bedroom Two-Story Barndominium - Main Floor Plan

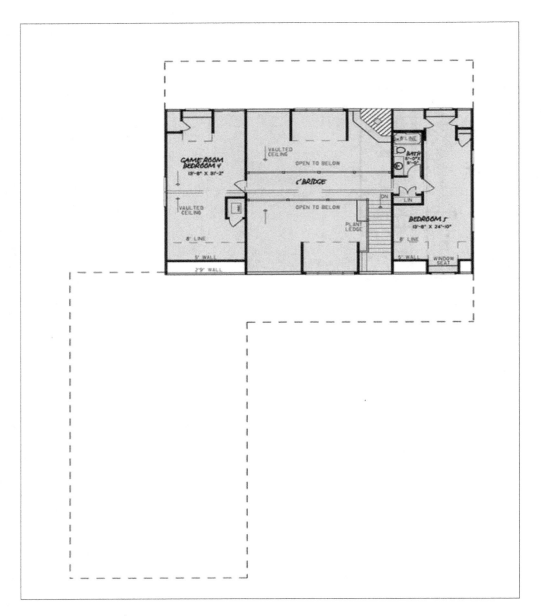

Gorgeous Five-Bedroom Two-Story Barndominium - Upper Floor Plan

With its covered porch, this L-shaped barndominium floor plan has a very charming rustic façade. A porch completely encloses the four-car garage. The master suite is situated on the first floor, across from the two guest bedrooms. The bedrooms are divided by the open living area, which has an amazing indoor-outdoor flow to the rear porch. The second level's final two guest bedrooms are arranged in an odd way with a bridge connecting them. The bedrooms themselves are fairly spacious and offer lots of additional storage space.

Best Floor Plans For A Modern Barndominium

Barndominium floor plans, sometimes called "barndo" floor plans, are homes with a rustic, steel-framed design that are reminiscent of barns. They offer well-built homes with all the contemporary amenities of a functional home, such as a unique outside design and a large garage or workshop area.

Originally intended for architectural purposes such as sheltering the farm's livestock, hay, grains, and fruits, barndominiums have developed into some of the most creative home designs.

The Evolution of the Barndominium

Not until Chip and Joanna Gaines turned a barn into a house in Fixer Upper's third season did the term "barndominium" and the idea of residing in a home with a barn-style exterior acquire popularity. The look attracted a lot of attention in Texas, Oklahoma, and other southern states before spreading to the rest of the country. It eliminated the idea of actually residing with horses and placed a garage/workshop in the center of the design.

Because builders and house plan designers noticed the affordability of this home style, barndominiums grew in popularity. Looking over the top 20 barndominium floor plans, you can see how they offer well-thought-out homes with great curb appeal and necessary features to accommodate any size family.

Condominium House Features

Barn house ideas are among the most creative and inspiring types of home designs. More and more people are choosing to live in barndominiums. They have a strong connection to the architectural characteristics of the Modern Farmhouse, one of the most well-liked house designs in the history of this sector.

Designs for Barn Houses Are Unique

When you picture converting a historic barn into a house, you probably picture the interior design of the house incorporating all the classic elements. Floor layouts for barndominiums mimic the distinctive characteristics of a traditional barn while preserving the character and charm of the architecture. Every one of our designs incorporates modern components to produce a warm and practical house. a combination of rustic siding, steel, and board & batten. These house plans are characterized by its rectangular shape, gabled roof, extended porches, and barn-style windows and doors. Our interiors typically have an open floor plan to mimic the spacious, light-filled atmosphere of a traditional barn. They also include extremely high ceilings, lofts, and decorative exposed beams.

The Dimensions of Barndominiums Differ

To satisfy homeowner needs, we provide a range of sizes for our barn house layouts. Slightly under 1,200 square feet is the size of the smallest barndo, for those who prefer a smaller footprint. At 4,913 square feet, the largest barndo is the largest.Depending on your preferences and your family's needs, a variety of house styles and features are available with the barndominium floor plans. Check out the best barn house plans below, for example, which contain the best designs, sophisticated features, and practical layouts.

The Best 20 Floor Plans for Barndominiums:

20. Design 963-00660, "The Chic Barndo"

One of the newest designs in the barndominium designs collection is the sleek Plan 963-00660. Large windows all around this unique house plan let in an abundance of natural light. With its black façade, this three-bedroom plan has 2,752 square feet, 2.5 bathrooms, an open concept living area, a mudroom, and an office.

19. Plan 5032-00140, "The Exclusive Barndo"

Plan 5032-00140. 18 includes an open floor plan, three bathrooms, five bedrooms, a loft, and an office.Plan 18. 963-00625 is "A Barndo Dripping with Sophistication".

Who would have guessed that "sophisticated" and "barn" would be used in the same sentence? Still, it's impossible to describe this house plan as anything less. Inspired by its three bedrooms, two bathrooms, separated bedrooms, open concept layout, loft, and office, the interior boasts isquare footage of beautiful finishes.

17. 963-00432 Layout: "Very Nice Garage!"

This barndo uses a variety of materials to improve its architectural façade and boasts an astounding 3,570 square foot garage! Plan 963-00432 also has cathedral ceilings, a loft, 2,776 square feet, four bedrooms, and three bathrooms.

16. Plan 963-00602, "The Sunny Barndo,"

One of the three-bedroom barn home ideas, this rustic beauty features a spacious sunroom with a cathedral ceiling and a fireplace. This floor plan has two bathrooms, an open concept living area, and a three-car garage.

15. "A Workshop and Barndo" (Plan 5032-00136).

Design 5032-00136 is a thoughtful floor plan with multiple distinct recreational areas and a garage workshop. This two-story barndominium has 2,765 square feet, two bedrooms, two full bathrooms, and a loft. For a close-up, personal look at the floor plan, check out our exclusive 360° tour!

14. Plan No. 963-00644, "The Rectangular Barndo,"

Plan 963-00644 welcomes you with a large covered front porch and makes a perfect rectangle. Cathedral ceilings adorn the inside of the house as well as the porch. Its 1,695 square foot interior also includes split bedrooms, three bedrooms, two bathrooms, and an open floor layout.

13. Plan number 5032-00117, "A Barndo with Garage Storage"

If you're looking for a well-thought-out barndominium floor plan with room for your boat or RV, this might be the plan for you. Plan 5032-00117 features an open floor plan, a huge wrap-around porch, three bedrooms, 2.5 bathrooms, a loft, and an office. Use our premium 360° tour to explore this 2,456 square foot layout and view the spacious 1,280 square foot parking lot.

12. "The Red Barndo," 8318-00115 as Plan

This one-story barn house plan is reminiscent of a classic barn with its rustic red color and large covered porch. featuring a 3,277 square foot open floor plan, five bedrooms, three and a half baths, and a mudroom in Plan 8318-00115.

11. The Plan 963-00387, "The Ranch Style Barndominium,"

This open-concept barndominium has unique glass garage doors and a covered patio with a wall of tall windows to let in natural light. This 2,079 square foot, two-story barndominium floor plan features three bedrooms, 2.5 bathrooms, and a loft. The master suite is located on the main floor. Additionally, 1,164 square feet are designated for the garage.

10. The Plan 5032-00152 is "A Barndo for an RV".

This industrial house plan is the perfect size for people who need space for an RV. In addition to having a half bathroom, the garage has 1,480 square feet of space. A wrap-around porch, a loft, a mudroom, three bedrooms, and 2.5 bathrooms are all included in the 2,311 square foot interior of Plan 5032-00152.

9. Plan 963-00601, "The Small Barndo,"

Plan 963-00601, a popular 1,460-square-foot floor plan, shows that bigger doesn't always mean better. Sometimes nothing but the fundamentals will do. Included are plans 963-00601, which have a garage workshop, two bedrooms, and an open floor plan.

8. Plan 9401-00114, "A Barndo with Outdoor Living Space,"

This gorgeous 2,486 square foot house plan utilizes every available square inch. No area is left unused with Plan 9401-00114's open floor plan, three bedrooms, 2.5 bathrooms, mudroom, outdoor kitchen, and study. View the 360° tour to learn more about this well thought-out layout.

7. Plan 041-00260 - "The Conventional Barndo"

Plan 041-00260 is a classic design that pays homage to small-town, nostalgic living. This two-story barndominium plan has a large 2,992 square foot home design with four bedrooms and three bathrooms, an open floor plan, a loft, and a mudroom.

6. "The Opulent Barndo" scheme, 6849-00064.

The incredible 4,357 square foot plan has several unique features, like a butler's pantry, a pet kennel, extra storage spaces, and a workshop. This barn home plan includes five bedrooms, an open concept living area, a movie room, a mudroom, a library, four complete bathrooms, and two half baths.

5. Plan No. 963-00411, "The Apartment Barndo,"

Plan 963-00411, the flexible floor plan for a 2-bedroom barndominium, is arranged as an apartment above a 1,554 square foot garage. One bathroom and two bedrooms are located on the top floor, which has an open floor design. The garage includes space for an RV and two cars, as well as a mudroom and a half bathroom. This style would be great as a primary residence, an investment property, or a great place to house needy adult children.

4. Plan 963-00627, "The Lakehouse Barndo,"

With its all-around windows and covered wrap-around porch, this two-story barndominium would make an amazing lake house. The 3,205 square foot interior features high ceilings, four bedrooms, 3.5 bathrooms, an open floor plan, a large bonus room, a loft, and a mudroom.

3. Plan 5032-00010, "The Metal Barn House Plan,"

Plan 5032-00010 is a popular choice among consumers because of its metal cladding and practicality. In addition to a guest bedroom, this two-story, 2,160-square-foot design features an open concept floor plan, a loft, four bedrooms, and 2.5 bathrooms.

2. "The Encircling Barndo" (Design 5032-00119).

This well-liked floor plan makes the most of the inside and outdoor living spaces. The front porch is easily wrapped around and has a cover! An encircling porch provides a great deal of space for outdoor living. Three parking spaces, a workshop with access to a half bathroom, and storage are also included in the garage. The 2,765 square foot interior makes excellent use of its features, which include an open floor plan, 3 bedrooms, 2.5 bathrooms, a den, and a loft. Get even more information about this floor plan by using the 360° tour!

1. Plan 5032-00151, dubbed "The Most Popular Barn,"

Plan 5032-00151, the best-selling barndominium, is masterfully built from a variety of materials with a touch of traditional scarlet. Along with an enticing wrap-around porch, this lovely barndo design boasts a spacious 2,123 square foot garage with ample room for a workshop and an RV bay. The inside has cathedral ceilings, an open floor plan, two bathrooms, and three bedrooms. This house plan also includes a loft over the garage and a different basement foundation. To see this barn floor plan up close, take a 360° tour!

A 360-degree image of Plan 5032-00151 within

In conclusion

Which of the top barndominium floor plans that you have now become aware of is your current favorite? The variety of barndominium floor designs is growing, with over 4,000 square feet of space available in addition to small barndo floor plans.

Chapter 2

How to Frame a Barndominium

The framing of a barndominium is a crucial step in the construction process that you might attempt to complete on your own. You may be able to frame the interior of your barndominium if you are a handy person.

Like in a typical house, the walls of a barndominium are often composed of wood. The procedure is a little different if you're building a barndominium as opposed to a typical house.

You will learn the fundamental stages required to construct a barndominium from this guide.

Assemble the external frames.

As a prerequisite to building a barndominium, the exterior frameworks must be constructed. Large steel frames are a common material for barndominium construction. Wood frames are fastened to the steel frame along the exterior margins of the interior walls. You need a wood frame in order for the drywall and the remainder of the inner frame to remain in place.

The flooring should be installed before you begin working on the internal frame. Place every frame on the earth. The frame is square-shaped and constructed from 2x4 or 2x6 boards. Eight-foot studs that have already been cut are added vertically, every sixteen to twenty-four inches.

Blocking prevents the studs from bending and provides additional strength. Wood fragments are placed horizontally between the bolts while blocking. Place the horizontal planks three or four feet below the bottom of the frame.

The frame is typically assembled in sections that are ten feet wide. You construct an 8-by-10-foot frame, hoist it up, and fasten it to the base and the steel frame surrounding it. Take a corner of the interior and start working your way out from there.

Embrace the windows and doorways.

Usually, extra 2x4 or 2x6 boards are used to add the frames for the windows and doors. The screws that hold up windows and doors are shaped to suit a rectangular frame. The outside siding and framework ought to have previously been trimmed to size for the windows and doors.

On the left and right sides of the door or window, new studs are installed. When installing window frames, studs are cut to fit a board along the bottom of the frame.

Construct the interior of the frame.

You can begin work on the interior walls after the exterior walls are framed. You'll probably use plans, which include information on the layout of the rooms.

It's always advisable to start in the living room's corner. Build the frames for the inside walls before moving on to the drawer and other feature frames.

Like the outer frames, the inner frames are often constructed on the ground. Raise the wall's initial frame and fasten it to the outside frame. Continue entering and moving through.

To build a mezzanine or second level, install joists.

Barndominium roofs are typically high and open, with only one storey. If you have a loft or second floor in your plans, you might need to install ceiling beams and joists. Joists are nailed throughout their breadth at the tops of the wall frames.

Typically, the upper level is supported by sets of two 2x4s spaced roughly 12 inches apart. There's flooring underneath the joists. Once the joists and flooring are installed, the interior walls of the upper floor can be framed.

Install fixtures for plumbing and electrical installation.

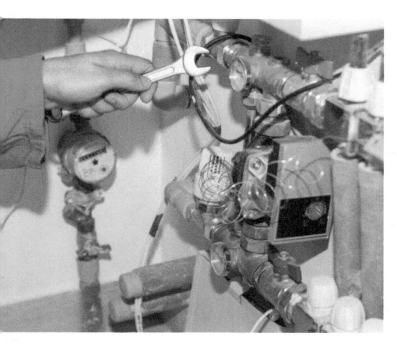

Fittings are required for the water and electrical systems. Plumbing components and electrical boxes must be included. The plugs frequently need to be placed in certain locations.

For example, you may need to check that every plug is between 12 and 18 inches above the ground. Furthermore, in certain locations, light switches must be installed 48 to 54 inches above the ground. Make sure to review the building regulations in your city before beginning any construction on the barndominium.

Complete the inside of a barndominium

The interior of the barndominium is completed to be framed once the fixtures are installed. To complete the inside, a few steps remain:

- Install insulation and walls
- Paint and cover the walls and ceiling.
- Install flooring
- Install the fixtures and appliances.

The walls and insulation are installed once the frame is complete. Batt insulation is the most easily installed type of insulation. Rolls that slide in between the exterior wall plates are how it's sold. Another option is to use fiberboard insulation that is trimmed to fit and installed into the wall spaces.

Before you can install spray foam or blown-in foam insulation, the walls must be hung. Additionally, you might wish to employ experts to install spray or blown-in foam. Care must be taken when installing both kinds of insulation to ensure that everything is covered.

Drywall is used to cover ceilings and walls. Hanging drywall requires starting at the top every time. To hang the drywall from the ceiling, you'll need two persons or a drywall jack. You must ensure that the drywall is correctly fastened to the ceiling joists in order to prevent it from breaking.

When hanging drywall sheets on the wall, begin at the top of the wall and arrange them horizontally rather than vertically. Do the top row around the walls before beginning the bottom row.

After the plaster is finished, you can install flooring or paint the interior. Painting the walls beforehand could lead to harm to the paint job while installing the floors. If you lay down the new floors first, you can get paint on them.

Appliances and fixtures are frequently installed last. These finishing touches include covering outlets and light switches, ceiling lights, ceiling fans, and appliances.

It's also typical to put off remodeling the bathrooms and kitchen until the frame is completed. The barndominium's shelves, refrigerator, and counters were just added.

How to Assemble a Barndominium's Frame

It may take several weeks to frame the interior of a barndominium, depending on the size of your floor plan. Since the outside walls will support the remainder of the frame, always start with them. When constructing the inner frames, begin in a corner and work your way around the walls until you reach the closets.

Should any of the tasks seem too difficult, you might wish to get help from an expert. Paying a little extra to hire someone else may reduce the likelihood of errors or defects. Even if you employ a builder, building a barndominium will still be less expensive than building a traditional home. This is due to the fact that well-built metal homes require less time to complete.

Options for Financing a Barndominium

Let's say you're looking for a cheap house outside of the city in the country. In that scenario, a barndominium—also referred to as a "barndo"—is the greatest option.

Typically, a barndo is a single-family modular home with an office or recreational space on the first floor, as well as a permanent basis for everyday living.

A barndo is self-sufficient due to its construction, drawing all of its energy from its walls. As a result, you can expand the second level for living or sleeping by erecting non-structural walls outside the shell.

Many people still cannot afford to purchase a barndo, despite the fact that they are less expensive than a traditional house. Because of this, financing is a crucial component of purchasing it, so you should consider all of your options.

Various Options for Funding a Barndominium

Purchase with cash

A few fortunate individuals can purchase their land with cash and not worry about obtaining financing in order to construct a barn. The benefits and drawbacks are listed below:

Advantages

- Your house is entirely your property.
- You can assess your risk-worthiness on your own without waiting for an investor to decide.
- Your credit score is irrelevant to anyone.
- You don't have to worry about interest rates rising when the market shifts.
- As long as you go by the zoning and construction requirements in your area, you are free to do whatever you want with your land.

Cons

- If all of your money is confined to your home, it may indicate that you do not have enough saved for other expenses.

Common loans for property purchases

You enter into an agreement with a lender based on your own abilities because a normal mortgage loan isn't guaranteed by the federal or state governments. Compared to other loan kinds, conventional mortgage loans typically feature lower costs and better interest rates.

Typically, eligibility requires a down payment and strong credit. If you have poor credit, however, you should be prepared for high interest rates and a sizable down payment.

Typically, a conventional mortgage allows you to borrow up to $650,000. The upper limit, however, is roughly $980,000 if you're developing in an expensive area. However, you can take out a larger loan if you receive a Jumbo loan.

Advantages

- Compared to other loans, these loans typically have cheaper interest rates.

- If your credit is good, you may be able to receive a mortgage that merely pays interest or that has a flexible rate.

Cons

- Having excellent credit is essential to get the greatest interest rates.
- Your credit score determines how much of a down payment you should make. If your score is low, a large down payment is required.
- There are no benefits associated with obtaining a mortgage secured by the federal government or a state.

programs for building loans

They are only valid for a brief period of time and have a higher interest rate than a standard house loan. It can be used, for instance, to pay a builder, purchase building materials, and purchase land.

To pay for the construction, you receive payments at predetermined intervals, and you only pay interest on the amount that you actually utilize. After the building phase is completed, the loan converts to a standard long-term loan with standard mortgage interest rates.

There are two types of building loans available:

Simply constructing things

This loan functions exactly as it says. It is only intended for land development. You'll need to locate a regular debt once the project is completed in order to repay the construction loan.

The fact that there will be two loans, two applications, and two closings is unfortunate. However, you are always free to shop around for the greatest credit offer.

Advantages

- Greater flexibility in selecting the most advantageous loan repayment plan.
- It is possible that during the construction of the house, the interest rates decreased.

Cons

- This financing only covers the construction portion.
- It's possible that while the house was being built, mortgage rates increased.
- There are two loans to discuss, and there are closing costs associated with each.

Constructing for Permanent

Because they just need to worry about one loan and one set of closing charges, the majority of debtors choose this loan. The builder, the building plans, and the estimate are approved by the lender prior to the start of construction.

Typically, only the money the builder withdraws at specific project milestones is subject to interest payments from the borrower. approximately every three to six months, roughly.

The loan becomes a regular mortgage once the building phase is complete and all of the construction funds have been utilized.

Advantages

- We are discussing a single loan.
- There is just one closing cost.
- That one lender will support you throughout.

Cons

- The agreement locks you in, and you are unable to obtain a standard mortgage from a different lender on more favorable terms.

FHA Loans

The FHA loan is a means of obtaining credit offered by banks and private lenders. Federal Housing Administration backs the loan. Through this program, low-to-moderate-income individuals, particularly first-time sellers, can receive assistance with home financing.

Everything you need to purchase a home is covered by the loan, including the land, supplies, labor, and building permits. An FHA loan is an excellent choice for those who are unable to make a sizable down payment because of its low 3.5% down payment requirement.

The debt-to-income ratio is stringent, but if you have savings or real estate, you may manage it.

Advantages

- A minimum of 3.5% must be put down.
- Those with high incomes but poor credit can still apply, as there is no upper income restriction.
- Open to those with poor credit. You usually require a minimum score of 580. On the other hand, you can still obtain a loan with a larger down payment if your score falls between 500 and 579.
- Suitable for many kinds of dwellings, including barndominiums.
- Even with poor credit, get low PRMI (Private Mortgage Insurance).

Cons

- In 2023, the maximum price you may pay for a single-family house is $472,030, or $1,089,300 in pricey real estate markets.
- An one-time insurance cost equal to 1.75 percent of the loan amount is required of you in addition to your monthly mortgage payments.
- An FHA loan can only be used to purchase your primary residence. You require a separate form of loan for vacation or investment properties.

- Strict safety regulations must be followed by the house you purchase, which might be challenging to do if the property needs repair. Before the building can be qualified, it must be inspected to make sure it satisfies the requirements. In addition, any issues must be resolved before the loan is approved.

VA Credit

Assume you have been in the military in the past or are presently serving. If so, you can use one of the home loans created especially for you by the Department of Veteran Affairs to purchase a main property or refinance your existing mortgage loan.

The VA appraises your property to make sure it meets their minimal property requirements. Once you have gotten all underwriter approvals, you can close the loan.

You must fulfill specific standards in order to qualify for a VA loan. But after you get the VA Home Loan Certificate of Eligibility, you can purchase the property.

Advantages

- VA loans do not require mortgage insurance.
- A down payment is not necessary.
- Interest rates are lower than those of a conventional loan.
- There is no required minimum credit score.
- VA loans allow a higher debt-to-income ratio, which makes it easier to buy larger or more expensive homes.
- The VA sets a maximum closing cost amount of 1% of the loan amount that a lender may charge.

Cons:

- There is a restricted type of property that you can buy.
- Manufactured homes need to undergo a structural engineering evaluation and are more closely inspected.
- The owner of real estate must reside there.
- The asset must be occupied as the primary residence.
- A home inspection and appraisal are necessary before to purchase. Because of this, a lot of sellers will turn down an offer from an experienced buyer.
- At closing, a financing fee must be paid. Typically, the cost equals 2.15% of the entire loan amount. However, if you are a surviving spouse or have a condition connected to your military service, you may not be forced to pay this tax.

USDA Loans

The US Department of Agriculture (USDA) has received government-backed home loans from numerous banks and other lenders. However, these loans are only available in a limited number of rural locations.

Low-income households can apply for a mortgage, which doesn't require a down payment. In addition, the application procedure is expedited.

Suppose you would want to build instead of buy. When that happens, it provides a construction-to-permanent loan, which is a single package deal that includes both a construction loan and a mortgage at the same closing fee. Usually, the interest rate falls between 3.75 and 7%.

The property must meet the following criteria:

1. A year-round access route to the land is required.
2. It must has a strong framework.
3. It must have a functional roof.
4. Plumbing and drainage systems must be established appropriately on the property.
5. There must be a functional HVAC system installed.
6. Its electrical system must be secure and dependable.

Advantages

• Loans that are guaranteed have no maximum.

- There is no upfront cost.
- The closing expenses might have to be paid by the seller. Invest in a property or refinancing an existing debt.
- Fixed, low interest rates apply to direct loans.

Cons:

- It needs to be the main home.
- It needs to stay in a designated spot.
- Your pay must fall into a particular range.
- There are upfront and one-time expenses.
- The house cannot be invested in for business purposes. However, it is possible to buy buildings that were previously commercial real estate.
- You have to choose a contractor who has been approved by the USDA in order to build a new barndo.

House equity loans

Assume that the value of your home loan remains. For that reason, you might use this as security for a loan to build a barndominium.

Advantages

- The interest rate on the loan is fixed and usually lower than other rates.
- An easy monthly payment schedule.
- You have up to 30 years to pay back the loan.
- You can do almost anything with the financing.
- It may be possible to deduct interest payments from taxes.

Cons:

- In order to qualify for the loan, you have to own a significant amount of your existing home and keep more than 15% of your overall value after the loan is paid back.
- Close expenses might range from 2% to 5% of the loan amount.
- If you already have available cash flow, taking on more debt may make it less.
- A reasonable ratio of debt to income.
- Get a credit score of 660.
- An excellent credit record.
- Demand proof of a steady job.

Individual Loans

You are able to take out a loan for any purpose with personal loans. The loan is repaid over a defined length of time with interest.

Generally speaking, depending on your credit and financial circumstances, the maximum amount you can borrow is $100,000 spread over 12 years. Personal loans have higher interest rates than secured loans because they are not secured.

For borrowers with credit scores greater than 760, personal loan interest rates are normally 9%.

Advantages

The advantages are as follows:

- You receive a lump sum at a fixed monthly rate, which makes payments easier to manage than with payday loans and other short-term loans.
- Personal loan approvals happen quickly. As a result, they come in handy when you need to get a big quantity of money quickly—usually the next business day.
- No assets, such as your home or vehicle, are offered as security for a personal loan. You don't have to worry about losing your home in the event that you are unable to make the payments.
- Compared to credit cards, personal loans have cheaper interest rates. The average interest rate on a credit card was 20.6% and the average interest rate on a personal loan was 11.29% as of August 2023.
- Compared to a credit card, you have the ability to apply for a higher loan amount.
- You can utilize a personal loan for anything. However, find out from the lender whether there are any usage limits before taking out the loan.

Cons:

- Because the loan is unsecured, failing to make payments will negatively impact your credit score and negatively impact your credit history.
- In the event that you are unable to repay the loan, a court may allow the lender to confiscate your possessions.
- Lenders will usually charge you high interest rates if your credit score is low.

- There are strict requirements to qualify for personal loans. As a result, if your credit score is low and your credit history is poor, you may have problems.

- Prepayment fines and other costs may significantly increase the overall cost of borrowing if you pay off the loan before the end of the term.

- A personal loan payment is another regular monthly responsibility, in addition to mortgage and credit card obligations. You may therefore find it difficult to stay within your spending plan and to make the necessary payments on schedule.

- Personal loans feature larger set monthly installments over the course of a specified loan period. Because of this, it's often more difficult to manage than credit cards that have a low minimum monthly repayment obligation and no late penalties.

Lenders Particular to Barndominiums

Generally speaking, barndos are categorized as factory-made modular homes that are erected on-site. Choose lenders who offer financing for modular homes, particularly for barndominiums.

Goods suitable for barndos can be found in the banks listed below. There are numerous options available, so explore and select the one that suits your needs. There is only one alphabetical order to the list.

Chase Bank (JP Morgan Chase & Co.)

Chase Bank, formerly known as JP Morgan Chase & Co., is one of the largest mortgage lenders in the US. Unfortunately, their products also need to meet the highest standards.

Generally, a minimum credit score of 700 and a 20% down payment. However, the company also offers reasonable loan rates to the selected applicant.

Furthermore, they offer financing for modular homes with a credit line, enabling you to make incremental payments to the supplier and builder. At the end of the construction phase, you convert the construction loan into a conventional mortgage, and interest becomes payable.

Fairway Independent Mortgage

Fairway Independent Mortgage is one of the largest lenders in the US. There are many things accessible for them, especially barndo kits. However, there aren't many goods suitable for buying land, and there aren't any options for financing development.

There are no down payments and credit scores above 580.

FMC Lending

Regardless of your credit score, FMC Lending offers things appropriate for a barndominium. However, if your credit score is low, you will have to make a down payment and pay higher interest rates.

While down payments usually range from 20% to 25%, interest rates normally range from 7.99% to 10.99%. It won't be too bad if this is limited to the first year of construction. However, if it is spread out over 15 or 20 years, it can become very costly.

Flagstar

Flagstar Bank offers a variety of financing options for modular houses, some of which allow you to purchase the Barndo kit and assemble it yourself. You can also buy the land. This organization offers barndo financing in all states.

The required credit score is at least 620, and down payments start at 3%.

Go Mortgage Company

Go Mortgage Corporation offers a way to purchase both your house and barn.

Based on your preferences and circumstances, a range of products are available for you to choose from. Furthermore, interest on your loan is not due until after the one-year build period has concluded and you have moved in.

A minimum of 640 on your credit score and a 3.5% down payment

Nationwide Home Loans

Nationwide Home Loans Inc. is among the greatest lenders for recently built barndos. However, they only make loans greater than $250,000. As such, it might not be suited for those who want to buy a Barndo kit and build one themselves.

However, they provide flexible construction loans with no interest until after you move in, and a 12-month build term.

Both an existing property and a modular home can be purchased with a loan. But you need to have a credit score that is better than 620. Conversely, certain products don't require a down payment.

Qualifications for Financing a Barndominium

You have to meet the requirements set forth by the lender in order to be eligible for an offer of a home loan. In general, going with a federally subsidized program will yield better terms than going it alone.

A list of the most significant requirements is provided below.

Credit Score

Your creditworthiness is a factor that lenders use to assess your degree of risk. Your credit score and credit history have an impact on how much you will respect the conditions of your loan and repay it.

A strong credit score of at least 650 increases the likelihood of loan approval for a lower interest rate.

In order to apply for a standard house loan, your score must be better than 620. Furthermore, the greater the score, the easier it will be.

If you use one of the government-backed programs, like the FHA, you just need a score of 500–579 for a loan with a 10% down payment. Alternatively, if a candidate has a score of 580 or above, the down payment is reduced to 3.5%.

Ratio of Debt to Income

Another need is to have a good debt-to-income ratio. The lender compares your income and debts to determine how easy you can afford the monthly installments.

Therefore, you have to prove that your pay both pays for your living expenditures and the increased debt.

Credit Reports

The three credit organizations that offer details about your previous debt obligations and payback history are Equifax, Experian, and TransUnion.

Lenders use these reports to evaluate your ability to repay loans on schedule.

Salary and Work Experience

You must provide proof of your income and employment. You need to show the lender that you can regularly pay off your payments each month.

Furthermore, the lender requires proof of identity paperwork. A consistent monthly salary or tax return, for instance, proves your eligibility to work in the country and your pledge to refrain from using the loan for money laundering.

Collateral

There are loan types that need collateral as a down payment, such as home equity loans. Typically, resources like savings accounts, cars, and real estate are used for this.

Interest rates on this type of loan will be lower because the lender is less likely to lose money on a secured loan than on an unsecured one.

A down payment

The majority of lenders need a down payment when a borrower takes out a loan. You can show the lender that you are serious about the financing and reduce the total amount borrowed by asking for a down payment.

If you intend to buy a property, the down payment for a home loan is placed into an escrow account managed by a real estate lawyer. After the sale is finalized, the funds are held in the account and given to the seller.

Evaluation of Real Estate

Before deciding how much to loan, a lender has to know how much your property is worth. This sum will be determined by the recent sales in the same location.

Before creating an appraiser's report, an appraiser considers the property's condition, location, and comparable home values.

The difficult aspect of purchasing a barndo is this. There might not be enough barndominiums in your area for the appraiser to make a valid judgment about their value because they are still a very rare kind of modular home.

Budget and Plan for Construction

A house loan lender must be aware of your meticulous planning, anticipated budget, and timeline for your new-build barndo project. After that, the lender will have a better idea of how much and how long you need to borrow money.

You have to look professional, hence your presentation needs to be good. Hire a certified architect or a contractor who has been approved by your lender to add credibility to your project.

Furthermore, the bank will know that your barndo will be built with skill if you choose a builder that has already worked with the lender.

Choosing the Right Barndominium Financing Option

To achieve the best value for your money, select the suitable barndo financing option from the relevant lender.

Some items to think about while picking a lender are included in the list below.

Customer service

You need to be informed of all the procedures involved in borrowing money.

As a result, find a lender that will interact with you and answer your inquiries clearly and succinctly.

Rates of interest and terms

Compare the interest rates, down payments, and loan terms that different lenders are offering.

Based on the information supplied, choose the loan that best suits your needs.

What fees do you have to pay?

As we already know, a home loan has costs and levies that go beyond just repaying the mortgage.

As a result, let us exercise caution with the following:

origination fees

These fees cover the administrative costs associated with your borrowing.

Commissions.

One group of third parties that get compensation are mortgage brokers.

Sometimes, lenders will pay for this. But usually, the borrower pays for it either as an added fee or as part of the repayments.

Costs associated with credit reports

The lender requires a credit report from one of the credit bureaus. This price covers the costs associated with this.

Again, this can be included in the monthly payback plan or paid for individually.

Discount points

A single payment made by the borrower can result in a reduction of their interest rate.

Proficiency

Selecting a lender who is unfamiliar with barndos in particular or modular homes in general is not a smart move. If you do, you will end yourself paying a high amount for an inferior product.

Lenders, not knowing about barndos, will defend themselves by offering ridiculous terms and rates just to be safe.

Authenticity

Don't go into this financial arrangement unprepared. It is crucial that you find out the lender's reputation.

Check through customer reviews as a consequence to ensure that they have a strong track record of satisfying customers and are conscious of what their consumers desire.

Choice of Loan: Advantages and Disadvantages

The following considerations must be made while selecting a finance option, such as a mortgage, in order to buy a barndo:

Home loans: fixed-rate versus adjustable-rate

It's simple to tell the two apart. Fixed-rate loans have fixed interest rates, and variable-rate loans have changeable rates.

Choose a variable-rate mortgage if you can afford a short-term loan. Additionally, if the interest rate is consistently dropping, it is better to choose a variable rate; if it is growing, it is better to choose a fixed rate.

Loan period

There isn't much you can do about a construction loan because of its fixed one-year short-term period. A home loan, meanwhile, can have a 15- or 30-year duration.

Choose a 15-year loan with a higher monthly payment if you can afford it. But you quicken the repayment of debt and the increase in equity.

However, a 30-year loan would be more suitable for those with lesser earnings because of its significantly cheaper monthly payments. However, greater interest rates and a bigger total amount are the outcomes of paying interest over a 30-year period.

Sort of Loan

Banks and other lenders offer a wide range of mortgage packages. Still, the mortgages that are listed below are the most popular.

- A commercial bank offers conventional mortgages based on the state of the market.
- Loans over $510,400 are classified as large loans. If you think this is something you should undertake, speak with private investors.
- The federal government incentivizes low-income households to acquire a part of mortgage loans. USDA, VA, and FHA are the current lenders of the back loans. If you meet the conditions, these home loans are worth considering because they are more affordable, some don't require down payments, and don't demand a high credit score.
- No-document loans do not need an applicant to have a normal credit score or provide proof of income. But the average person might not be able to afford the interest rates and down payment. Furthermore, not many lenders offer these.

A down payment

It is advisable to make a down payment as large as possible, despite the fact that some individuals may find it difficult.

As a result, you incur lower debt and interest rates.

Penalties associated with early payment

If you are able to pay off your home loan early, there will be a penalty assessed by the lender. The penalty allows the lender to maximize interest income by incentivizing the borrower to spread out the principal payments over an extended period of time.

The interest you were able to avoid paying is frequently equal to the penalty. As a result, early loan repayment is rarely necessary.

A Successful Barndominium Financing Application: Some Advice

To improve your chances of being approved for your Barndo home loan, make sure you follow the guidelines listed below.

Correcting errors in your application can speed up the submission process and improve the chances of it being accepted.

Find the best lender.

Financing a barndo construction is not the same as obtaining a conventional home loan.

Choose a lender with experience in agricultural or modular building and who is knowledgeable with barndominium properties.

Create a solid plan.

Since it demonstrates to them that their money is in skilled hands, the lender loves to read a concise, unambiguous report outlining your needs for the funds.

A strong plan has to include as much detail as possible about the project you wish to create, the projected cost of building, the timeline, and the contractor you wish to collaborate with.

Make it look like you are an expert by including charts and images. If you present this data in a stylish report that satisfies your requirements, you'll be halfway there.

Assessment of properties

To determine the value of your land and finished project, speak with a qualified property appraiser.

Insufficient barndos in the area could make it tough for the appraiser valuing your finished home. But don't give up.

Can you obtain a mortgage?

Find out how much you can afford to borrow before looking for a loan, a house, or a barndo kit.

When your bank or credit union looks into your income and credit history, they can tell you how much you can afford to repay.

Federal home loan programs

Verify that you are eligible for any government-backed home loan program you intend to select.

If you are not eligible, you cannot participate in the program, no matter how much money you have.

Boost your credit standing

Pay off the obligations you now owing, focusing on the bigger ones.

This will increase your residual income as well as your chances of getting a loan authorized.

Increase your income and savings

If you can, consider moving, getting a better paid job, or taking up a part-time job to help you out financially. Increasing the value of your present savings through a high-interest savings account is an additional choice.

Try to reduce your expenses at the same time. Perhaps hunt for other vacation destinations and cut back on the luxury.

Choose a lender who has funded the purchase of a barndominium before.

Many lenders specialize in barndominiums or modular homes, especially in rural areas.

Try some of the lenders in this book, or contact government home loan programs such as USDA, which can provide a list of approved lenders. Next, get in touch with as many of them as you can to see if they finance barndominium purchases.

Get any papers ready that may be required.

Get a copy of your credit report, then check it for errors and omissions. The number of people that hold false information would astound you.

So straighten them out as soon as possible. The lender will receive your credit report, but they will also need supporting documentation to dispute any errors that might still exist.

Combine all the supporting materials for your application into one document to make it easier for them to read. If you make things easy for the lender, they will often do the same for you.

Work together with an experienced barndominium builder

assemble the résumé and relevant references of your preferred builder. Check to see if they are authorized to work in your state, and if so, provide copies of their insurance bond and license.

If you hire a builder that has worked on government house loan programs before or who they already suggest, the lender will be more at ease.

Responses to Frequently Asked Questions

Typical questions consist of the following:

What is the typical cost of building a barndominium?

In 2022, the average cost to build a 2,400 square foot barndo was approximately $300,000. Barndos ranged in price from $120,000 to $540,000. The source of this data is HomeAdvisor.

How much down payment is needed to finance a barndominium?

Depending on the type of loan, the lender, the building location, and whether the loan is guaranteed by a federal program, different down payments are needed for mortgages for barndominiums.

A down payment of 20% or more of the entire loan amount is often required by the majority of lenders. Conversely, VA home loans do not require a down payment.

Is it possible to rent out a barndominium?

A barndo could be rented out in theory.

Actually, though, this depends on the financing needs and terms of the mortgage.

How long does it take to have a barndominium's financing approved?

If everything is in order and there are no delays, you should expect to hear back from the underwriter within 45 days regarding the acceptance of your mortgage application.

Can someone with weak credit receive a barndominium loan?

Individuals with low credit ratings can apply for house loans from a number of mortgage organizations. On the other side, budget for high interest rates and a substantial down payment.

Alternatively, you can obtain a mortgage with a credit score of 500 if you qualify for one of the federal government home loan programs; some even waive the down payment requirement.

Next Actions

In order to qualify for a loan for a barndominium, you need to have the following:

- A solid credit history and score.
- A suitable debt-to-income proportion.
- Sufficient funds for both the down payment and closing charges.
- Verification of a steady income.

As an alternative, benefit from the superior lending terms provided by federal home loan programs backed by the VA, USDA, or FHA.

Some homeowners believe that financing a barndominium is difficult. Still, it's the same as getting a conventional mortgage. Providing you take the time to familiarize yourself with the requirements of the various lenders offering barndo financing options, submitting your application ought to be a breeze. Why don't you take action now?

Chapter 3

Things You Should Know About Building a Barndominium

Living in a barndominium could be ideal for you if you enjoy being outside and anything that resembles a barn.

Tell me now about a barndominium. It's a massive structure that can be either an open-concept steel building constructed from the ground up or a residence converted from a barn. Typically, these types of buildings are constructed on large tracts of land in rural locations, but they are also beginning to appear in non-urban settings.

Compared to traditional wood-framed buildings, barndominiums require less care, are easier to construct, and last longer. They can be constructed more quickly and affordably.

However, you should do some research before jumping in and getting to work, whether you're building on an already-built barn or a brand-new kit. These are the key points of building a barndominium that you should be aware of.

1. Get your project approved.

Obtaining the necessary permissions is an essential for anyone beginning a building project or renovating to ensure everything is up to code. Permit costs vary from $400 to $2,000 depending on your location, so budget accordingly if you plan to build a barndominium.

Your local building and safety agency will likely have codes governing the dimensions and design of your structure in addition to instructions on where to put septic tanks, how to wire them, and how to handle plumbing.

Don't assume that just because a barn is on a house that you wish to buy, it was built legally or with the necessary licenses. Find out what modifications you are allowed to make to your barn by speaking with the local planning office.

2. Examine the paint.

When repairing an older barn, it is crucial to ascertain the type of finishes that were applied.

According to Matt K., lead paint may be present in windows, walls, trim, siding, and other areas of older barns constructed before 1978.

These areas should be inspected prior to work commencing as they may sustain damage during the restoration. If the test is positive, Kunz adds that depending on the size of the barn, the cost to address the issue might be very costly.

3. Prepare for unforeseen expenses

Building or renovating a barn for habitation is far less expensive than building a traditional home. Unexpected expenses will still surface during the construction process, though.

Remember how much it will cost to clear the property and prepare it for construction. It may also be necessary for you to lay a new foundation. The price range for this might vary from $5,000 to $30,000 based on your location and the kind of footing you require.

You're converting an abandoned building into a habitation, so you'll need to budget for modern amenities that will give it a homey vibe. Items like as washing and dryer connections, tile or hardwood floors, and HVAC systems fall under this category.

4. Create an electricity work plan.

For an ordinary barn, electricity is not something that needs to be considered. However, since a barndominium need power to function, it's critical to consider the type of energy it will require from the outset.

The power requirements of all the lights and appliances that will be installed in the house should be examined by a licensed and professional electrical company, which you should hire. Additionally, the provider ought to guarantee that every wire is just where you want it to be.

According to Sean, "It takes a lot more work to fix things after the Sheetrock or walls are up."

Selecting the right lighting and installation techniques can be challenging, so plan ahead to ensure that your options will be available when it comes time to install. You may also choose to include security lights or devices, thermostats, and smart doorbells in your makeover.

Modifications to a project after the contract is signed might be costly.

5. Choose your windows and doors carefully.

High energy bills are frequently the result of drafty windows and doors. Additionally, choose windows with two or three panes and front doors made of heated steel or fiberglass to prevent an increase in your energy costs.

Glass Doctor president Brad Roberson advises adding a sliding glass door to your plan so you can enjoy life indoors and out and allow in more natural light.

"When looking for a sliding glass door, look for features designed for energy efficiency, such as double-pane glass and composite gaskets," advises Roberson.

6. Installing soundproofing is crucial.

Because barndominiums are constructed with steel frames and metal walls, they are not very excellent at maintaining a constant temperature. They have the ability to gain and lose heat throughout the year.

Experts advise using batting as insulation or foam boards, insulated panels, or spray foam insulation to increase the heat resistance of the affected areas.

Large Black Barn A 5700-square-foot barn with dwelling quarters is located in Oklahoma.

Building barndominiums is becoming more and more popular, so those who are interested won't have to worry about when to plan or begin construction. When barndominiums initially became popular, it was difficult to find manufacturers and secure funding for them. Many of today's builders are also well-versed in barndominium construction. People who own barndominiums would make excellent clients for interior designers as well.

Sit down and savor your tea or coffee. The Large Black Barn The house we're presenting you today, Oklahoma Barndominium, will wow you. You will find nothing to dislike about this barn-style house. Three living areas, a complete bathroom with a walk-in closet, and a balcony are located upstairs. Most of the barn is in the basement. There are 5700 square feet of covered space on the first floor and second floor.

It is also owned by a builder and a designer couple along with their small family. That's fantastic. Is there anything better?

Outside of Oklahoma Barndominium

Family members refer to it as "Big Black Barn." This home is a refuge. Brett McPherson, Tray's wife, planned it and he built it. Certain external elements, such as the posts, beams, windows, and barn door, retain their iron ore hue. It's quite the difference!

Before you enter, you'll pass through the patio where the family frequently congregates. The owner can read a book, sip coffee on the porch, or simply relax while watching the kids play in this comfortable space. This area already gives you a hint as to the owner's preferred style. The willow furniture looks extremely rustic with pops of color from plants, toss pillows, and a few unique accessories.

Front door of a black barn

This house's floor layout is incredibly practical, especially considering that the owners designed the barndo themselves. You enter a tiny kitchen as soon as you enter the Big Black Barn Oklahoma Barndominium living area. It will be convenient for those who work in the barn not to have to go upstairs. It's modest, but it's fully equipped with a fridge, microwave, and even an ice maker, adding a more contemporary element to the Scandinavian design we'll see more of upstairs.

The brown polygon-shaped floor tiles, white backsplash and tabletop, and black storage cabinets all blend together beautifully. Fun color and pattern pops attempt to draw your attention on various kitchenware.

Just next to the door, around the corner from the tiny kitchen, is a space to stash filthy boots and horse helmets. A restroom is also located in this location, directly beneath the steps. The barn's alley is accessible by another door.

We ascend the staircase.

If you were pleased with the designs below, get ready to appreciate every shade, pattern, and detail that the next level has to offer. More fantastic design inspiration can be found in the Big Black Barn Oklahoma Barndominium. And every single component has a tale to tell.

Who doesn't enjoy stories, after all? Every house has a story to go with it, which adds to its uniqueness. You'll hear some of those stories to truly get a sense of the love and effort the owners have put into this lovely home and to inspire you.

Start with the stairs. Brett enjoys attending every one of them since everyone is so proud of their steps. Through a large window, a plenty of light enters. Brett bought the picture beneath the window as his first piece of art. Among the many things he adores about this compact area is this. And there will be a pile of photos in another corner of their newborns donning headdresses from India.

Not to leave anything out, the landing of the stairs is enhanced by these exquisite floor tiles. We'll then discuss the interior's extra-white paint job, which gives the entire space a dazzling appearance.

Let's go on to the main living space now!

Right through those stylish batwing doors, you can enter. From here, a sizable open area connects the dining area, living room, and kitchen. The second-floor living area of the Big Black Barn Oklahoma Barndominium is 1780 square feet, in addition to an 80-square-foot balcony. The living area downstairs, including the kitchen and bathroom, is 2100 square feet.

Let's begin to appreciate beauty more now, shall we?

The kitchen

You're welcome to take your alone time. Observe everything. We have the same thought. This eco-friendly kitchen is amazing. It's not large, but it has the perfect amount of space with black stainless steel appliances (wait until I tell you about the cabinet tower in the corner)!

Yes, I am aware of it. The wall's tiles. The open shelves and the lighting. The window and the black farm sink. The tints! Friends, nothing to say. Breathe deeply a few times and swoon!

Brett discusses her fond memories of the kitchen, including the black sink. Her children craft on the white quartz counter every day. Open shelves are practical and have a nice appearance, therefore I like them. Because these make it so simple to grab items and put them away, we adore this concept.

Your life will be saved by the tower to the right. The most functional cabinet in the entire kitchen is the one she uses to store the baby bottles, coffee maker, and other items. P.S. Paper plates, glasses, and pots & pans are kept in large drawers. There are rollouts all over the lower level that allow you to remove a tiny, thin cabinet for baking sheets and a spice rack.

The dining room is in one corner, and a door opens to the balcony.

Living Space

There are two spots in this stunning home where I can only exclaim "wow" or "OMG." Not concocting this. There won't be much left to say about these patterns and compositions.

Your eyes will dart from one thing to another since there's a lot of white space. Every piece is worthy of recognition. It incorporates elements of Native American and western design as well as a variety of Scandinavian designs. Look closely at the head mounts, Pendleton patterns, tooled leather, and vibrant western arts!

On the other hand, a few items in the Big Black Barn Oklahoma Barndominium truly stand out and have interesting histories. For instance, to create this exquisite one-of-a-kind sculpture, the chandelier's proprietors collaborated with two antler design businesses.

Those stunning Oklahoma Barndominium doors from Big Black Barn surely also pique your curiosity. Every door is custom-made from slab doors with edges cut to fit and moldings attached. Everything is a source of excitement, including the handles on the Kudu barn doors.

Have your eyes already been pleased by these exquisite pieces? Another one is this one! The green enormous swivel chairs that were custom-made for the room served as inspiration. These are exactly as comfortable as they appear, according to their owners.

The room is completely white, which makes it appear to go on forever and be extremely light. Include the light that the dome emits. The worn-out and aged-looking knotty wooden flooring is what draws your eye in. Everything, even those lovely rugs, is something we can't get enough of.

sleeping rooms

Now, let's head to the private rooms. The structure will eventually serve as the center of the company, albeit it will take some years. That makes three rooms with beds in them.

The main bedroom, which measures 16 by 15, has a half-vault in the roof. The master bedroom in the opposite room is exactly duplicated in the girls' bedroom. The room across from the master bedroom is the baby's room.

The design of the rooms is on par with that of the entire house. Because of its distinctive components, the room serves as more than just a place to sleep. Some of the walls are a basic white color, while others have darker and softer earth tones mixed in. Particularly in the master bedroom, the artwork on the walls is a fantastic accent that complements the drapes.

Perched atop quaint, tastefully crafted bedside tables are the intriguing bedside lamps. They are practical as well as beautiful. The bed is composed of standard white sheets that have been enhanced in appearance with Pendleton furniture. The way the room's colors and accents complement each other so perfectly makes it impossible to take your eyes off of that gorgeous grin.

The lavatory

Of course, new concepts continue to be developed by individuals. The Big Black Barn Oklahoma Barndominium's restrooms include the same exquisite features as the rest of the living area. This also holds true for doors that are customized for you. The bathroom looks modern thanks to the floating drawers. The room has a rustic atmosphere because of the saltillo tiles.

The mirrors are quite heavy and custom-made for you as well. It would be interesting to share the tale of how they "nearly burned the house down" in the process of hanging these mirrors. By mistake, they bore through wires and turned off the electricity.

To put this up, a number of different things took three or four days. These lovely products are definitely worth the effort. Might also inspire us to take any necessary steps to get the desired look!

The countertops are made of obsidian marble, while the plush bath mats are made of sheepskin. The bathroom should have a traditional style with a touch of western design. Pendleton towels and a creative western towel hook will help you accomplish the western appearance.

The vaulting design in the shower is still extremely nice, even though it's a little different. The shower tiles, however, have a more sophisticated and traditional appearance.

The Outbuilding

Downstairs is where the barn is. There are four stalls, runoff stalls, a lean-to, a wash rack, a tack room/office, a workshop with additional hanging storage, and a porch. The stall gates resemble the batwing doors upstairs, and the barn features large ceiling doors. These Dutch doors lead to the alley. There is a drive-through lane in the center of the barn that can accommodate a full-sized truck and trailer.

Even if it's a barn, you may still enjoy making it feel a little homey. The barn's sitting and reading areas are great places to unwind.

Chapter 4

Cozy Converted Barn Barndominium with Loads of Style

Although barndominums are designed to be houses, many of them are constructed to resemble barns. This may cause you to question if it's a good idea to convert an old barn into a dwelling. After witnessing this adorable and fashionable converted barn barndominium, you can make up your own mind about whether or not converting a barn is a good idea.

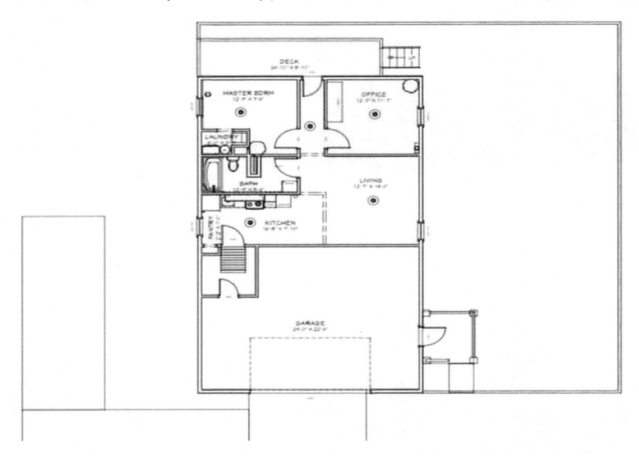

The garage and the outside

This barndominium's exterior still has a barnlike appearance. The building is rectangular, long, and straight, with a gently sloping roof. Huge garage door taking up one wall. There are a few windows and an entry door on each of the other walls.

This barndominium retains its authentic barn-like appearance because to its muted red color. The addition of a deck to the wall across from the garage door is the sole exterior modification made to this barndominium. It is surrounded by a lot of old trees, which lends the place an air of timeless beauty.

The garage is fairly basic, with just a wooden partition separating it from the rest of the house. It can accommodate two automobiles or a large amount of tools, household goods, and other objects.

The wall that divides two rooms and provides access to the other areas of the house is called a door. The simple design consists of an overflowing cup, several wood cutouts of beer bottles, and vintage street signs. Additional decorations and items that need to be stored are kept in a few floating boxes.

Living Space

The walls are decorated with prints, the living room has a suede couch that wraps around the room, and there are baskets scattered throughout for various home goods. The clean, soft gray walls, which are almost white but not quite, contrast beautifully with a gorgeous, glossy hardwood floor.

The guitars and records that hang on the walls are proof that the owners enjoy music. Uncovered ductwork is deftly concealed by a door. The silver ducts complement the soft gray walls nicely.

Guest room or office

With a large clothing rack visible on one side and a desk and chair on the other, the office and guestroom are incredibly functional. Wire boxes hold many types of papers and other rubbish.

During the day, the straightforward single bed in the center of the room doubles as a couch thanks to its abundance of large, plush cushions and blankets. The space is united by a little palm tree and some paper stars that are suspended from the ceiling.

This room is modest but functional thanks to the brick accent wall and the heavily colored green walls on all four sides. The result is a very stylish design. A large Persian area rug colors one wall.

The window wall is a perfect area to store various papers that need to be accessible because it is equipped with corkboard panels. There are also some adorable floating shelves and a dry-erase calendar housed in an artistically designed frame in this section.

The eating area and the kitchen

With an open floor design, the kitchen and living area of this barndominium are seamlessly connected. It's a terrific option to do some light writing or have breakfast quickly to sit at the bar facing one wall. It also aids in creating a wall dividing the kitchen and living room.

The floor's transition from wood to tile is another feature that helps set them apart. In a kitchen lacking in counter space, you can use this bar area as an additional surface. Still, the kitchen looks good.

The nearly black cabinets contrast beautifully with the light gray walls and ceilings. Above the sink and counter is a bright red shelf that holds various glasses and other culinary supplies.

This room's light-reflecting wave wall behind the sink looks fantastic. The area has a hint of modern-rustic flair thanks to the attractive yet basic white tile counters. There isn't much storage space in this room without a built-in pantry because there isn't a closet.

The kitchen and living room windows are situated directly across from one another. This provides both rooms with natural light.

The bedroom

With a straightforward metal bed frame that is exposed on all sides, the bedroom is really basic. To provide depth to this area, an oval form behind the headboard has been painted as an accent. The orange-and-copper blanket draws inspiration from the rest of the house and complements the headboard's shape.

This color is also found in the Persian rug underneath the bed. The throw pillows on the bed and the rug's blue accents complement each other. The ductwork in this area is visible and elegantly wrapped. It crosses the room to reach the opposite side from the door. The silver's pleasing light reflection makes it appear fantastic with the light gray paint.

A charming barndominum converted into a stylish apartment

If you've ever considered what you could do with an old barn, this adorable residence should inspire you. They will cherish their first house for a very long time because it is theirs. The Barndolife ebook has tons of inspiration for creating your own haven inside a barn.

Ideas for Barndominium Interior Design

Barndominiums have gained a lot of popularity in recent years, making them a fantastic option for those who adore the style of rustic rural houses and spaces.

Every barndominium has unique features, and you may customize it to your liking with a little effort. These structures house a large number of second-home owners. Though tiny homes and small-scale living have gained popularity recently, barndominiums continue to pique the imagination of both younger and older people.

Realize your aspirations for a home.

You can use these 26 barndominium decorating ideas as inspiration for interior design and decoration.

1. **Basic Beauty**

Ideas for a barndominium living room that highlight the rustic appeal of the refurbished barn can help you create a sense of harmony in your living area. The barn room is exquisitely illuminated by minimalist white design components.

The getaway's timeless traits are primarily its straightforward design and rustic materials selections. The stark white paint on the slat walls contrasts sharply with the dark timber floorboards.

2. **Basic wooden barn doors**

Traditional wooden barn doors can be used to go up to the living area as part of a barndominium's architectural concepts. These are a fantastic, all-natural substitute for conventional French doors. They let in plenty of natural light and fresh air without taking up any additional space.

To give the exterior style, incorporate a few basic black features. They give the all-white space some form without being overly cluttered.

3. Intelligent and Varied Character

A modern spin on a traditional country barn is one concept for a barndominium design. Maintain the space's lightness and airiness by using shiplap walls and white draperies. The vivid pattern contrasts with the warm, muted hues that are often found inside a barn. The ambiance of a room can be delightfully simplified with wooden barn doors.

4. Innovative Uses of Barndominium Decor

Try combining furniture with both metal frames and natural materials when you're decorating a barndominium. You may create a wire shelf unit similar to those found in farm-style decor out of a wire basket.

Your room's focal point can be a large, straightforward wall clock. If you want a more rustic vibe, exquisite silver boxes resemble galvanized buckets. Plants and other greenery can breathe life into a space.

5. Barn lofts with metal ceilings

Instead of altering the classic barndominium's charm, make the most of its architecture and structure to create an absolutely ideal space. The lofty ceilings prevented the interior wood from appearing cramped and drab.

You can make a center area in a barndominium for conversation by adding barn lofts. The traditional hardwood design is given a more rustic appearance by the metal railing. Many empty spaces in the ancient barn could be put to good use in a contemporary barndominium.

6. The kitchen of a barndominium

A spacious kitchen is a crucial component of a barndominium house. For a more rustic vibe, consider incorporating butcher block worktops and bar stools into your kitchen. You may add some color to your bar stools.

The counters showcase rich wood tones that are mirrored from the beams throughout the country home. You may be able to add a barn loft to your kitchen, giving it a more unique and historic appearance, if your roof is vaulted.

7. Allure of the Nation

A kitchen-to-living room open floor layout might add coziness, warmth, and style to the barndominium. Open flooring, typically found in barns, are a great way for homeowners to divide up their spaces.

White wooden planks on the walls of the lovely barndominium, together with the exposed rafters, might provide even more intrigue. The space feels more spacious and airy because of the high ceilings and abundance of natural light coming in from the windows.

8. pastel aqua hues in a fresh style

Light, muted blues blend well with cold colors, so add some ease to the decor of your barndominium. It looks more intriguing and more like a traditional rural cottage thanks to the blues and greens. There are numerous creative ways to incorporate style and increase the use of a trunk and wire basket for storage.

Traditional country homes frequently have these kinds of timber components. Your rustic space will feel happier and more airy with some plants in it.

9. **calming burst of color**

The walls of a classic barndominium can still be painted a different color. Although wood panel walls are necessary, you can modify them somewhat to create a more contemporary, serene, and calm atmosphere. There may be some squishing in the living room because the beams are below the roof. Paint the ceiling and beams white to create a feeling of richness and airiness.

10. Log fireplace in the barndominium

Your living room's focal point will be a natural fireplace with a traditional mantle. The fireplace contributes to the barndominium's rustic appeal by adding charm and coziness to the space. Natural light enters the space through the windows and the walls' vibrant colors. To make the other items in the room stand out, avoid overdécoring the space.

11. Expand the appearance.

Open floor plans are common in large barn conversions, especially in the family area and kitchen. These kind of rooms use light-colored schemes throughout, from the furniture to the ceiling. The room appears larger and more airy due to the monochromatic design. Open shelves and light-reflecting glass cabinets are features common to rural kitchens, such as farmhouse country kitchens.

12. Barn is full of warm, rich hues.

The colorful bar stools and the throw blanket's warm, rich hues complement each other beautifully when the cushioned furniture in light colors is added. The space appears larger when the glass shelves are positioned in front of the window. Numerous windows throughout the barndominium allow in plenty of natural light and fresh air.

13. The Lodge Design's Appearance

Barndominium decoration ideas employ a classic lodge style to create a comfortable and pleasant residence. It's thought that a barn with a variety of wood tones feels deeper and more airy. A barndominium's floors, ceilings, beams, stairs, and cupboards are all composed of wood.

In order to avoid having an overly complex design, this person may utilize a variety of wood types or paint the wood in different colors.

14. A barndominium's loft

A typical barn loft overlooking the common area of the kitchen can be converted into a traditional rustic sitting room. The darker kitchen table contrasts beautifully with the floor's lighter gloss.

Still, you don't have to remove the large barn elements in order to use the area. Actually, they can provide more depth and character to the area. An overhead pendant light can give a traditional barndominium a contemporary feel.

15. Old-looking stone and wood features

If your barndominium already has wooden floor planks, adding a rural wall to the living area will make it seem more vintage. It will look fantastic to build an archway between the living room and bathroom and center it with a classic rural fireplace. All of the barndominium adheres to its central principle of light, open mobility, and straightforward design.

16. Wooden flooring in the bathroom

Hard floors are perfectly OK for bathrooms; they're just easier to maintain. Applying additional varnish coats to the wooden floor is one method of doing this. To protect the hard floor, place a bath mat down that can absorb a lot of moisture.

17. Door doubles on the barndominium front

Barndominium double front doors are a common choice when decorating the interior of these rustic spaces. The room has a rustic atmosphere because of the way these doors merge in the middle to create a sunburst motif. They are often made from rough-hewn wood. The paneling on the barn doors and trellis complements the aged wood with an olive green hue.

18. Wooden neutrals that are gentle

The unique rustic barndominium style effectively showcases New England home furnishings. Allow the aged, weathered wood to complement the delicate gray hue of the wooden furnishings. You might opt for a more subdued tone of gray on your wooden floor as opposed to the warm orange tones that are typical with barndominiums.

A floor-to-ceiling fireplace with a wooden beam mantel will give your barndominium a rustic character.

19. Enhance the room's lighting with pendant lights.

The cathedral-style beams will assist you in harmonizing with your home's long lines. These beams draw attention to the traditional barndominium's soaring ceilings. Your home can gain coziness, light, and warmth by having ceiling lights hanging from the ceiling.

Another option is a folding kitchen door, which will add a contemporary element to your home's traditional design. Large windows will give the space a lighter, cleaner, and airier sense. Arrange rustic furniture around it to bring in more wood to your living area.

20. Elevate the area in your kitchen.

Choosing a large table over a kitchen island is a great way to elevate the country vibe of your traditional kitchen. Consider purchasing a table with an open bottom and carved legs when you are shopping.

Keeping functional and decorative copper pots and wire baskets out in the open can be quite beneficial. Use dark to neutral color tones in your kitchen to add interest to a neutral color plan.

21. What are the fundamental characteristics?

Typical components of a traditional barndominium are steel frames and sheet metal. To make it resistant to these elements, you can install a sheet metal roof. The dark wood siding contrasts beautifully with the white frame windows.

To give the space an air of sophistication, keep things straightforward and uncomplicated. Forms with straight lines and tailored shapes are encircled by warm natural components. Install a built-in corner shelf with the wood still on it to keep everything unpolished and organic.

22. Contemporary rustic furniture

Use a rich design style that blends bright colors with dark wooden beams to give the house's structure a more intriguing appearance. There are several of gorgeous red-hued hardwood flooring that you may install.

The bedroom's twin barn doors, painted gray, complement the room's white woodwork and walls. The pendant lights add a sense of mixed-style rich rustic richness to the space.

23. Sustainable Barndominium

It is feasible to construct a sturdy, environmentally responsible home with classic barn elements and an industrial steel wire-railed barn loft. If you design the spiral staircase yourself, it can be made to match the available space.

Bring the raw, industrial aesthetic indoors. The rooms can be divided with a divider constructed from repurposed steel roofing components. The air inside will remain clear and bright if there are lots of plants and trees.

24. aged natural materials

Accept the inherent beauty of worn and aged objects. A welcoming veranda with windows can be created by combining long stone walls and reclaimed wooden board ceilings.

Without overly adding to the room's woodiness, a lighter-colored painted wooden plank floor will assist create the atmosphere of a rustic, classic barndominium. White leaf-patterned pillows can give the space a refined appearance and some pattern.

25. Natural and Earthy Components

Use these guidelines to learn how to decorate your barndominium. An elegant fireplace surround and a half wall made of fieldstones will give your barn a contemporary appearance. You may choose to use an existing beam that has served another purpose for the top.

Place antiques and gold accent pieces, such as pots, dishes, and an iron gate, atop the mantel. Your barn will seem rustic with walls the hue of red and a stone base.

26. Reclaimed Architecture from a Barndominium

Your living space might benefit from the aged and worn appearance of peeling and chipping building debris. For a rustic look, use window frames that have chipped paint and aged, rusty sheet metal siding.

With a large fireplace, a red wooden floor, and a soft braided rug, the luxurious barndominium living area will come to life. To complete the space, add industrial bar stools and a stunning pendant light.

Barndominium Exterior Ideas

Constructing a barndominium could be something to consider if you're looking to purchase a new home. It's understandable why barndominiums are growing in popularity. They are far less expensive but still offer all the advantages of conventional residences. Furthermore, you can modify them to suit your preferences and needs.

Have a look at these stunning barndominium exterior designs if you need some inspiration. They're fantastic!

Gorgeous barndominium exterior design ideas that you will adore

Building barndominiums is becoming more and more popular, so many builders are searching for distinctive exterior designs to set their projects apart. If you're merely interested in what's trendy right now, or if you're a builder like them, here are some options.

These stunning outside designs for barndominiums are worth considering whether you are starting to build a new one or are just beginning to look at them.

The most beautiful exterior designs for a barndominium

Having a siding

There are numerous siding options available, and each offers advantages of its own. Whatever you decide, adding some color or texture will make your house stand out. Alternatively, you may wish to select items that will be fashionable in a few years. Among them are:

- External aluminum walls
- Installing stucco
- Ribbed metals
- Boards made of vinyl

The following are some fantastic colors for your barndominium siding that will improve the appearance of your house from the outside:

- **White:** Classic colors like white give everything a nicer appearance.
- **Beige:** this is a fantastic shade to tan without looking yellow. Beige is a color that is growing in popularity for exterior home design, despite the fact that not everyone enjoy it.
- **Brown or bronze:** This hue goes well with the many bushes and plants that surround the house.
- **Dark gray** is a fantastic color that complements all other hues. Dark gray goes well with nearly every color of trim.
- Black is a terrific option if you feel that dark gray isn't dark enough. **Black** is a color that never goes out of style or becomes dirty.

Whatever siding color or texture you choose, as long as you love it, is irrelevant. The outward appearance of your house reflects your interior feelings.

Ceiling

Considerations for selecting a roof include cost, ease of maintenance, and available color variations. Metal, clay, and shingle roofs are available. A roof can enhance a home's exterior. While painting and landscaping your home's exterior can greatly improve its curb appeal, metal roofs give the entire property an outdated appearance. They come in a variety of colors, complementing any style or design, and have a lengthy lifespan. Consider using clay tiles if you wish to avoid the noise that a metal roof produces.

Clay roof tiles are among the most widely used roof tile types worldwide and have been for 5,000 years. Clay roof tiles are more expensive than other roofing materials, but they will last longer.

With the help of solid knowledge, take all the time necessary to ensure that you select the ideal roof for your house.

Outside Kitchen

The outdoor kitchen is a place where people may get together with their loved ones. You can roast chicken for a winter holiday gathering or grill salmon on a summer night. Having a built-in BBQ space of your own makes entertaining guests simple and enjoyable.

Consider your intended usage of the area as well as what you can see from your house when designing an outdoor kitchen. Verify that the items you use and view within it bring you joy. It's useful to have an outdoor kitchen, and you'll be happy you invested the money to add one to your barndominium.

Landscape

Making landscaping improvements is one of the best ways to enhance the appearance of the outside of your house. If you plant some native trees and bushes, your house will appear nicer than it has in a long time. Given the high cost of landscaping, it's not necessary to complete the job all at once. Start little and gradually add more.

The inherent beauty of your yard can be enhanced by the addition of a pond. This is something you might want to add onto your house if you have a lot of land. You and your family can enjoy a pond for many years to come, and building and maintaining one isn't too difficult.

Columns

The columns in your house may support the structure and look fantastic from the outside, particularly if you add masonry and stain them to match any color scheme.

Patio

Is there somewhere to unwind outside your barndominium? If so, it makes sense to build a patio onto the exterior of your barndominium. You may even convert the patio into a full-length covered porch encircling your home. This provides plenty of space if you wish to set up seats and tables outdoors!

Numerous windows

Your home will appear nicer and you will be able to appreciate the outdoors more if you add large windows. Larger windows also let in more natural light, which enhances the brightness, vitality, and welcome feeling of any space!

The fireplace

While brick chimneys are one style, there are also attractive metal chimneys available. They're a fantastic method to showcase your unique likes and style in your house! Adding a chimney to your barndominium outdoor ideas is a terrific idea.

To sum up

If you wish to customize the exterior of your new project, you should consider using at least one of these stunning barndominium outdoor ideas. Regardless of the one you choose from our list, you will adore having your new place called your own.

Large Tennessee Barndominium with a 2600 square foot living area and a large glass-door garage

The Tennessee barndominium's exterior

One of the best things about barndominiums like this Tennessee one that we chose is that the living room and even the garage can be really huge. This exterior, which is warm white and iron ore in hue, begs the question, "What's inside?" The outside of this stunning house appears nearly black and white at first glance. Its scale is belied by its simplicity.

A wraparound porch is a great feature for entertainment purposes. The natural color of the Cypress wood used for the posts makes the outside look even nicer. Antler chandelier that precisely fits the wood posts lights up the entrance. The porch is kept bright throughout thanks to the barn lights.

In addition to matching the color of the roof, the black window and door trimmings look fantastic against the white wall. The arrangement of the front windows is unique.

The Garage

The outside living area is extremely beautiful, but the drive-through 40x50 garage with ceilings as high as 14 feet is what you really need to see. Aside from being incredibly spacious, what makes it fascinating is that it has glass doors, something we haven't seen many barndos with. Making sure there is a lot of natural light inside without having to open the garage doors or the lights is a terrific idea.

Inside of a Tennessee barndominium

There are 3 bedrooms and 2.5 baths in this huge Summertown barndominium. As soon as the doors open, you stare immediately into the kitchen. Also, if you're a friend, something must be cooking for you, so please come in. The kitchen isn't extremely huge or sophisticated. In a small kitchen, you'll need things like stainless steel equipment, ample storage space, and a backsplash that matches the colors. The whole thing is warm white. Of course, the hue of the rock in the middle is also extremely attractive.

You will be shocked at how much space there is in this big house when you go into the barndo.

In front of the kitchen, there is a huge veneer stacked stone fireplace with gorgeous white shiplap walls. The concrete flooring are gorgeous and appear much like real wood floors. The stained pine wood canopy that ran across the whole mezzanine is a magnificent feature.

The roof of a barndo is 18 feet on the sides and 24 feet in the middle. This makes the inside light and airy, and the wide glass doors and windows let you see the outdoors quite clearly. Ceiling fans are also set up to make sure air travels freely within.

Level Two

From the balcony, you have a full view of the downstairs living space, the large fireplace, and more of the exterior. Like the first floor, the second floor is also rather spacious. There are two bedrooms and a communal bathroom on this floor. Or perhaps you could have a second living room.

Sleeping rooms

The master bedroom is located on the ground level, in the hallway behind the kitchen, while the other bedrooms are above.

The master bedroom features shiplap walls, vinyl "wood" flooring, and a stunning pine ceiling.

Toilets

Shiplap ceiling and walls in the bathroom match those in the main bedroom. The bathroom features two sinks and a large tub. The shower room's ceramic tile wall looks fantastic. This bathroom seems very elegant because of the black water fixtures and the chandelier in the center. Who can resist a gorgeous shower head, anyway? Having it in the shower is so awesome!

In the center, accessible from both beds, is the upstairs full bathroom. Two sinks, one at either end of the bathroom, are also present. The bathroom wall's material, which is more like fiberglass and acrylic than tile, helps a lot with cleaning. Given that children use the restroom together, this is crucial.

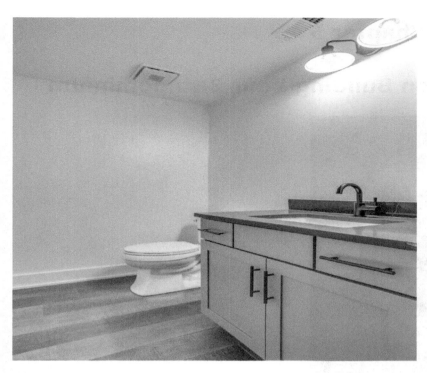

The Brief and Acronymous of It...

Constructing the barndominium of your dreams can be challenging at times. You will run across issues and become irate along the road. To make it happen, especially if you want to avoid making any mistakes, you must have courage, tenacity, and guidance.

In the long run, purchasing a barndominium for your family is well worth the cost.

Chapter 5

Mistakes to Avoid When Building Your Barndominium

If you intend to build your own Barndominium, you are definitely aware of the benefits and drawbacks of these unique structures. Building a Barndominium requires careful planning despite its simplicity.

The following are the top 12 faults you should steer clear of when building your barndominium to ensure its longevity:

1. Not Doing a Budget Calculation Before Starting Construction

Running out of money in the middle of a project can be inconvenient, especially if you don't have any other funding sources. All you're left with is an incomplete, unlivable house.

Before starting construction, make sure you have a clear grasp of your financial situation to ensure you have enough funds to pay for your entire Barndominium.

2. Observing Site Activities Before Construction

All buildings are built on foundations, even barndominiums. Before building a foundation, the site must be properly prepared; leveling the ground and ensuring that it can sustain the foundation and the structure are important tasks that should never be overlooked.

3. Not Making Any Upgrade Plans

Barndominiums can be purchased as useful kits. On the other hand, a set number of doors, windows, and other components are included with these kits. If you want to install extra windows and doors, you will have to order more supplies.

This increases the overall cost of building a Barndominium; when estimating the cost, keep these details in mind.

4. Creating Your Own Floor Plan Drawings

Construction of your own Barndominium offers greater freedom in terms of plan and design.

You can change the floor to suit your needs. Although you can design the floor plan on your own, working with a qualified constructor is essential because of other important factors. They include elements like air conditioning, heating, natural lighting, and structural support. The amount of living space is greatly influenced by the size and arrangement of each room as well as the hallway.

5. Poor Choice of Land for Your Barndominium

If you don't already own the land where your barndominium will be built, you may need to look for a suitable residential neighborhood with laxer building rules.

Wisconsin barndominium ideas, for example, are more effective in rural than in urban environments. When developing a barndominium, factors including property size, nearby properties, security, road access, and ease of access to amenities are taken into account.

6. Selecting the Wrong Contractor

A skilled builder can help to expedite the entire building process. One advantage of hiring professionals is that they may help you save money and prevent mistakes.

Even while most contractors are reliable and sincere, others see projects with ulterior motives. Making the wrong contractor choice could result in increased costs and project delays.

7. Underestimating the Height of Your Barndominium

For example, a two-story Barndominium is higher and can accommodate more rooms. Certain local governments have restrictions on the highest building height allowed inside their boundaries.

Depending on the limitations, a higher Barndominium may require a lower roof pitch. The frames of these structures have a significant impact on the height that can be utilized for further floors. Please confirm that the frame size and available area will allow for a two-story Barndominium.

8. not establishing a completion date.

You must determine an approximate completion date for your Barndominium building, whether you want to do it yourself or employ a professional builder.

Without one, your project can take longer to finish, increasing the cost of building. Together with the expert you hired, set a timeline and work toward meeting it.

9. inadequate insulation on the roof and walls

The predominant materials used in barndominium construction are metal sides and steel frames. These materials absorb heat in the summer and lose it in the winter. A comfortable room temperature must be maintained during the winter months if you insulate your home enough.

10. Not Confirming the Building Codes in Your Community

Different locations have different building codes, therefore it's crucial to confirm with the local authority. Obtaining approval may be required before you can construct your Barndominium. Avoid making the costly error of not checking or breaking the building codes in your community as this can lead to fines.

11. Failure to Provide Overhangs for Large Windows and Doors

Eaves and gutters take most of the rainwater away from the foundation of your Barndominium. Unfortunately, they don't provide enough security for your property.

Rainwater may cause your Barndominium frame to flood and collect around it if it isn't built on an elevated foundation. Your foundation is weakened over time by soil erosion. Consider adding an overhang over large windows and doorways to protect your property.

12. Taking Care of Everything by Yourself

Building a Barndominium is a significant do-it-yourself project. It is recommended that you work with an expert unless you have enough expertise overseeing major projects. During construction, things can go wrong quickly if specific jobs are not completed by experts.

Small mistakes added together could eventually result in bigger problems. Installations involving plumbing and electricity require qualified workers. If you try to manage things alone, you will run into a number of problems.

To sum up

There's no denying that creating a barndominium is usually simpler and faster than building a traditional residence. They are significantly more sturdy and come in kits that make assembling them easier.

You ought to know which are the top 12 blunders you might make when building your own Barndominium after reading this book. By avoiding many mistakes, you can save time and money on the constructing process.

Constructing a Colorado Barndominium

Building your own home will be among the most difficult things you have ever done. However, over time, it may also prove to be one of the most beneficial. While not everyone has the chance to create a home that is built exactly how they want it, for those who do, the time and work involved can be well worth it. However, you already know how much labor and effort it takes to build your own home if you've ever done any research on the subject. It can also be extremely expensive, making it unaffordable for many people.

Building a barndominium in Colorado can therefore be a very smart decision. Because it is less expensive and simpler to construct, you may build the house of your dreams without having to go through all the hoops you would normally have to. Sales of barndominiums are rising along with the alternative housing movement, and more banks and builders are starting to enter the market. Because of this, now more than ever is the ideal time to think about building a barndominium in Colorado.

This chapter contains all the information you might possible need to build a barndominium in Colorado. If you follow these recommendations and make sure everything is planned correctly, you may be able to build the house of your dreams much more readily than in the past.

What Is a Barndominium and What Are Its Advantages?

A barndominium is a home built on top of a pole barn or metal post-frame structure. These kinds of buildings are usually used for commercial or agricultural uses, such stables or storage, but they may also be used to build beautiful homes that you can customize to meet your exact specifications. If you framed the outside of the house like you would an ordinary one, you would never even know that the structure was made of non-traditional materials.

One of its main benefits is that establishing a barndominium in Colorado can be substantially less expensive than building a standard home. A barndominium is built in approximately half the time of a conventional home. This is due to the fact that the buildings are easier to frame up after the concrete slab base and poles are driven into the ground and cement-secured. Because constructing is so straightforward, you may save a lot of money on both labor and supplies.

Another advantage of building a barndominium in Colorado is its durability. Steel cladding and posts are resistant to mold, mildew, and decay, which makes them ideal for use in barndominium construction. These things might cause problems in a traditional house in a state like Colorado where snowfall is frequent. Nevertheless, using a barndo could eventually result in lower repair costs.

Cost of Building a Barndominium in Colorado

Once you have made the decision to build a barndominium in Colorado, you should think about your budget. The simplest method to do this is to calculate the cost per square foot of your construction. One advantage of doing this is that you will be able to calculate how big your concrete slab foundation should be and how much house you can afford. Next, you can decide how many bedrooms and bathrooms you need, as well as where you want them situated in the house.

Building a traditional home in Colorado costs roughly $136 per square foot. It's important to keep in mind that this sum just covers the initial construction of the building. It excludes furnishings and finishes, which you will need to buy individually with money taken out of your budget. This can make the cost of your item more than you can afford.

The cost of building a barndominium is substantially lower in Colorado. Building a barndominium in Colorado typically costs $108 per square foot. With the money you saved, you might be able to purchase a custom-built home that fulfills all of your housing desires. With this extra money in the budget, countertops, cabinets, electronics, and furniture may all be bought.

Colorado Builders of Barndominiums

After you have decided on a budget for your Colorado barndominium, you will need to think about who you will hire to finish the construction. Depending on the builder you select, your barndominium project may or may not succeed, but if you can collaborate with someone who genuinely cares about your demands, you will be able to feel secure during the entire process. In the building sector, there are many various kinds of builders, therefore it could be difficult to select the right one for your project. Thankfully, there are a few telltale signs you can watch out for to make sure you're making the right decision.

When beginning a barndominium project in Colorado, the first thing a builder should have is experience with metal post frame constructions. Finding a builder with prior expertise constructing this kind of structure is essential, as not all builders will have the skills required for this specific project. The process is unique, and it takes skill to execute it well. If at all possible, look for a builder with experience doing this kind of job.

You should also look for a builder who has a good track record of providing excellent customer service. It's critical that you get along with your builder and confirm that they have the experience necessary to put you at rest. To help you get started and choose the best barndominium builder in Colorado, we've put together a list of some of the best.

Construction with Drop Tine

Despite being a relatively new firm, Drop Tine Construction's objective is supported by the fact that all of its builders have past building and construction experience. Their deep roots in the community make them a great choice for building a barndominium in Colorado.

Sunset Structures

The majority of Sunset Buildings' clients is repeat business. This shows that they are capable of offering their customers high-quality goods and support, so it's quite likely that they will be able to do the same for you.

Pregio Homes

PregioHomes

Because of their dedication to the Colorado barndominium construction process, Pregio Homes is skilled and knowledgeable. Since the core of their business is their constructing approach, they can easily and quickly deliver a building that is precisely created to meet your needs.

Colorado Sources for Barndominium Kits

If building a Colorado barndominium from the ground up isn't your thing, there are other options available to you, including a barndominium kit. The prefabricated barndominium kits are already completely completed when they get to your construction site. For that reason, they are an excellent option if you don't want to take your time gathering the materials for your build.

Barndominium kit suppliers will help you every step of the way throughout construction. Some of them even provide recommendations for builders who have already finished their kits. This suggests that you will always receive the support you need, no matter what stage of the project you are at.

Colorado Banks for Communities

Community Banks of Colorado takes the time to learn about you and your objectives in order to find the perfect loan for your particular circumstances. They are really focused on the community and have a very strong connection. If you want to work with a bank that will help you, they could be a great choice.

Southern Colorado Farm Credit

Farm Credit of Southern Colorado offers loans for your Colorado barndominium as well as for other projects. You and your partner will decide on the best conditions for your project as well as your needs regarding the loan's length and interest rate.

Taxes on Colorado Barndominium

Just as with any other kind of property, your Colorado barndominium will require property taxes to be paid. However, certain barndominiums are regarded as dual-use construction by the IRS. This suggests that various areas of your property, including the storage and living spaces, will have varying tax rates applied to them. See your local tax assessor to find out how much you should be paying in taxes.

Where in Colorado Can I Find Barndominium Insurance?

No matter what kind of home you own, insurance is always a good idea. Not even your Colorado barndominium will be an anomaly. It is important to always confirm that your barndominium has emergency coverage. This can sometimes mean that in order for your insurance to cover things like flooding or wildfires, you will need to add extra clauses. Find out how you should be covered by speaking with your local insurance agent.

Colorado Barndominium Floor Plans

One of the most important components you will assemble for your Colorado barndominium is the floor layout. The layout of the house, including the bedrooms, baths, and living areas, is specified in the floor plan. Make a list of everything you would like to incorporate into your floor plan before you begin. Next, have a skilled draftsman look over that list. They will use it to create a useful floor plan that you and your builder can use to construct your Colorado barndominium.

To sum up

After reading this essay, you should have a firm grasp on the conditions necessary to build a barndominium in Colorado. By knowing what to expect at each stage and what you should be doing beforehand, you may speed up the project.

Chapter 6

Modern Farmhouse Plans with Barndominium Style

Are you looking for a place in the country to call home? View these contemporary farmhouse plans in the barndominium style, which mostly features wood frame (though the term "barndominium" is often used to describe metal constructions). Board-and-batten siding, spacious kitchens, and quaint porches all exude a classic yet modern feel. These are eleven visually arresting examples.

Barndo in Style with Covered Porch

Barndo Style Wraparound Porch (1064-111) - Front Exterior

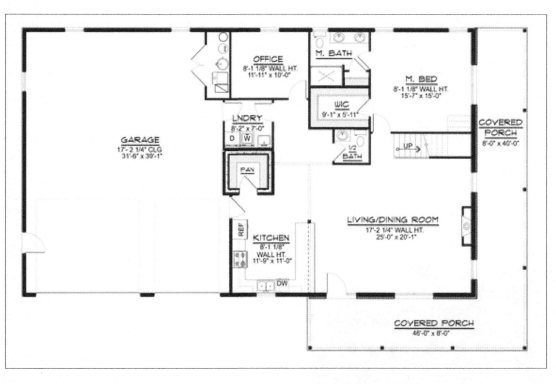

Main Floor Plan 1064-111 in the Barndo Style with a Wraparound Porch

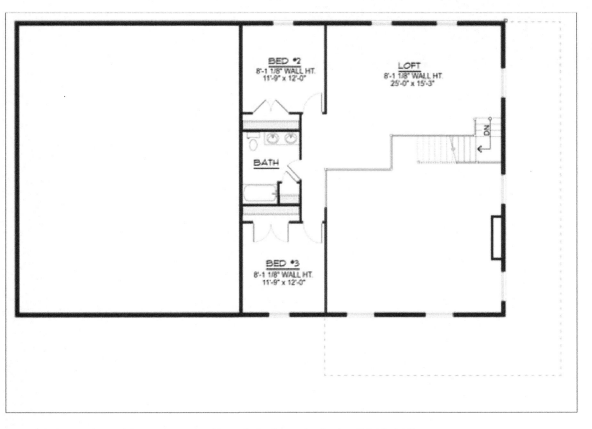

Upper Floor Plan with Wraparound Porch in Barndo Style (1064-111)

113

This modern farmhouse design is in the barndo aesthetic. Our favorites are the elegant wraparound porch and the aluminum gable roof. The primary living spaces are connected by an open floor plan in the interior design, which makes the area feel spacious and serene. Look at the home office and the spacious garage.

The master suite is on the main floor to facilitate aging in place. Two secondary bedrooms above share a full bathroom. Don't forget about the flexible loft.

Workshop and Three-Car Carport

Workshop 1064-148: Three-Car Front Exterior Garage

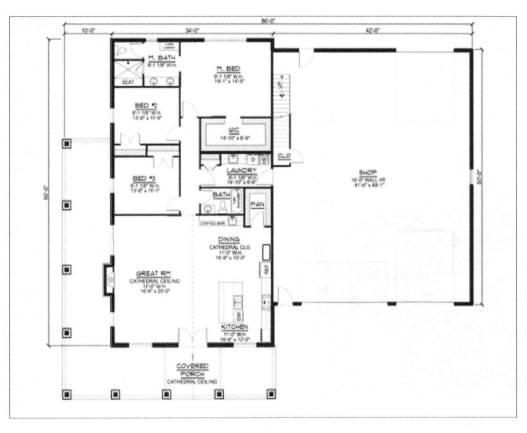

Main Floor Plan (1064-148) for Three-Car Garage with Workshop

Plan 1064-148: Upper Floor of a Three-Car Garage with Workshop

The wraparound porch on this modern farmhouse style significantly increases its curb appeal. Observe the roomy three-car garage and workshop as well; these are charming elements of a barndominium. You want to relax as you gaze out over the living area from the spacious kitchen island.

The spacious walk-in closet in the main suite facilitates easy maintenance of clothes organization. An movable loft and a storage area round out the second story.

Ample Kitchen Island

Large Kitchen Island - Front Outside 932-521

Main Floor Plan 932-521 - Large Kitchen Island

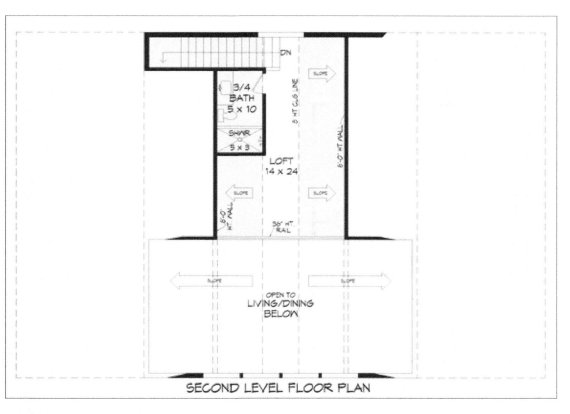

SECOND LEVEL FLOOR PLAN

Big Kitchen Island - 932-521 Upper Floor Plan

Check out this barndominium house idea. There is a fantastic kitchen island with seating for seven that opens to the living room and dining area. It also has an eating bar. You'll appreciate the convenient walk-in pantry and the large, adjacent mudroom/laundry area.

A high workout room and studio area are nice bonuses. The upper floor has a loft and a bathroom with a shower.

Basic Farmhouse

The front facade of a small farmhouse (124–1263).

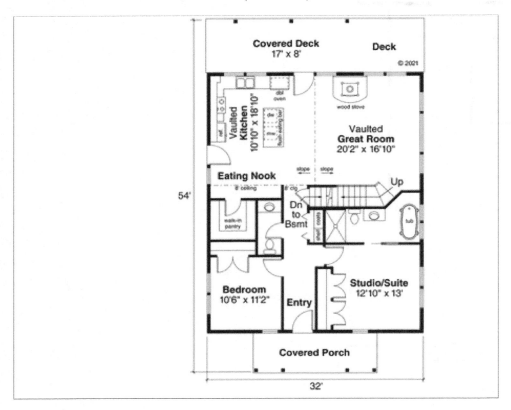

The modest farmhouse's main floor plan is 124-1263.

Basic Farmhouse 124-1263: Initial Floor Plan

This lovely rural house blends classic farmhouse elements like board-and-batten siding, a gable roof, and a welcome front porch with a modern floor design. The large area features a high ceiling and a wood burner. A well-equipped kitchen has a walk-in pantry with cabinets, a central island, and a flush dining bar.

The main suite and one more bedroom complete the main floor. Upstairs has more versatility thanks to a full bathroom and loft.

Salutations Spirit

Congenial Environment 430-259 - Front Exterior

Warm Ambience: Main Floor Layout 430-259

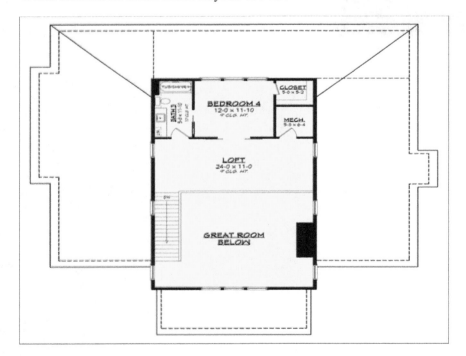

Comfortable Ambience 430-259 - Initial Floor Plan

This modern farmhouse design has stunning board-and-batten siding for a rustic curb appeal, as well as a quaint front porch. The practical arrangement allows for easy access from the kitchen to the dining area and great space. The large pantry has ample space for everything.

The split-bedroom design affords the main suite plenty of privacy. Additional features include walk-in closets in each bedroom, a spacious back patio, and a handy loft.

Practical Floor Planning

120-274: Ideal Floor Plan - External Front

Main Floor Plan 120-274: A Practical Layout

This farmhouse design exemplifies the barndominium style with metal frames. The country kitchen comfortably flows into the family room, with lots of counter space. Nestled at the rear of the arrangement, the master suite offers privacy along with a spacious walk-in closet, two sinks, and a safe area.

The two secondary bedrooms are located close to the front of the house and each includes a walk-in closet. Beside the door, a study offers a quiet place to work. The spacious covered patio at the back is our favorite spot.

Simple Life Outside

Front exterior of Simple Outdoor Living (1074-24)

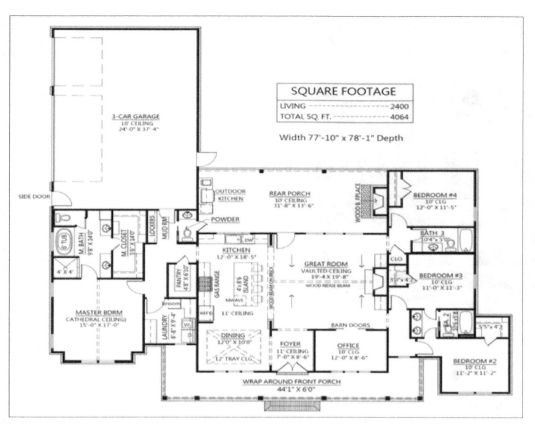

Featured Floor Plan: 1074-24 - Easily Live Outside

The traditional wraparound porch and gable roof of this farmhouse set it apart. The modern interior decor is both fashionable and useful. The dining area and the great room are entirely connected to the island kitchen found in the major living spaces. The master suite features a spa-like bathroom and a spacious walk-in closet.

A must-see is the elegant drop zone by the three-car garage, complete with lockers. The home office provides privacy in a chic way with barn doors. nice and sunny weather? Savor the best of outdoor life on the kitchen-equipped back porch with a wood-burning fireplace.

Small-Scape Farmhouse Plans

Front Facade of 430-282 Narrow-Lot Farmhouse Plan

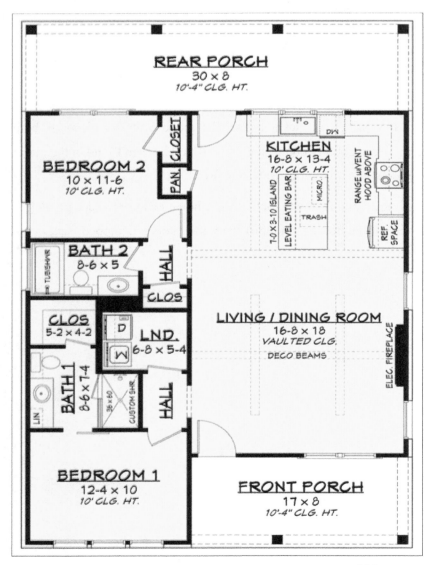

Main Level Layout for 430-282 Narrow-Lot Farmhouse Plan

With its open layout and effective use of available space, this creative farmhouse plan is ideal for a small lot. The kitchen's level eating bar makes it simple to service the living and dining rooms. With front and back porches, outdoor living opportunities are increased.

The master suite, an additional bedroom, and a full bathroom complete this arrangement.

Light and Modern

Modern and laid-back 1074-44 - Front Exterior

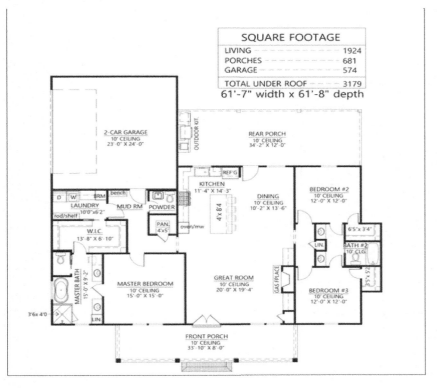

Modern and Airy-Main Floor Plan 1074-44

This farmhouse style perfectly captures modern living. The kitchen and the great room are connected by an island. The front and back covered porches of the home provide shade. The main suite, which is situated on the left side of the plan, offers direct access to the laundry room.

On the opposite side are two further bedrooms with walk-in closets and a combined full bathroom. In the mudroom, a seat has been provided so that you may take off your shoes.

Plans for a Two-Level Farmhouse

Two-Story Farmhouse Design with a Front Exterior (923-273)

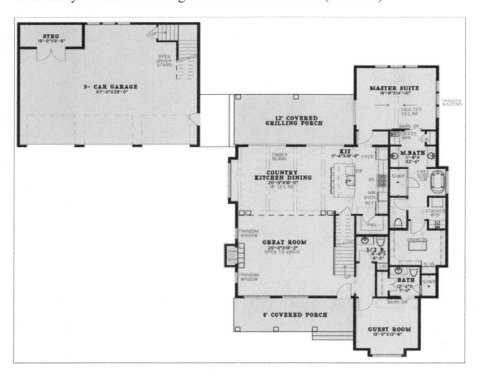

Two-Story Farmhouse Design: Main Floor Plan 923-273

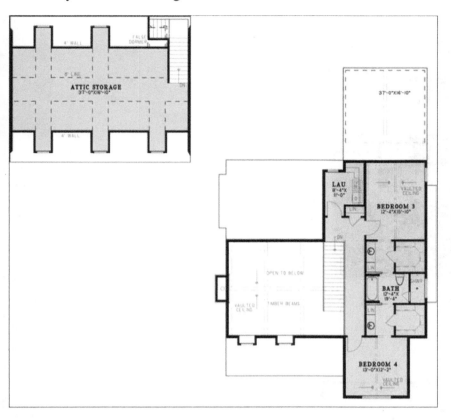

Two-story farmhouse with an upper floor plan, design 923-273

This two-story house plan quickly grabs your attention with its farmhouse-style exterior. There's an air of openness and carelessness inside. Take a look at the kitchen, which features a sizable island that comfortably seats people. Sliding doors open to expose a covered back porch.

The luxurious amenities in the exclusive main suite include a coffee bar! A guest suite is located close to the layout's front. Two bedrooms are connected by a Jack-and-Jill bathroom on the second floor.

Ample Storage Capacity

Many Storage Spaces - Front Exterior 51-1213

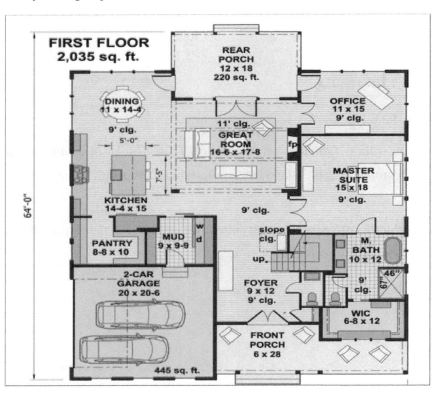

Main Floor Plan 51-1213 - Plenty of Storage

Ample Storage (Floor Plan 51-1213, upstairs)

This farmhouse plan with four bedrooms greets you with a large front porch. The centerpieces of this gorgeous design are the open kitchen and great room, which feature an island that makes it easy to serve meals here and to the dining area. The mudroom and walk-in pantry add useful storage.

The main suite's amazing bathroom, complete with a calming tub and an oversized closet, is not to be missed. An office with access to the back porch is located in the back of the layout. Three more bedrooms, a loft, and two baths round out the second story.

Floor Plans for Barndominium

In recent years, barndominiums—so named because, well, they look like barns—have garnered a lot of attention.

While most people think of "barndominium" as referring to metal structures, we define barndominium as any type of structure that maintains the look of a barn. This expands the category to include floor plans with wooden framing that resemble ideas for pole barns.

Designers of barndominiums have been coming up with more inventive concepts lately. The modern barndominium is one of the most intriguing and varied architectural categories of the year. It comes in a range of floor plans, from spacious open floor plans with modern facilities to cozy cottages.

It could be difficult to select from the numerous features and specs offered in this design area. Thankfully, we are pleased to present to you the floor plans for the barndominium that we already enjoy.

Minimalistic Barndominium Floor Plans

Front exterior of a simple barndominium floor plan

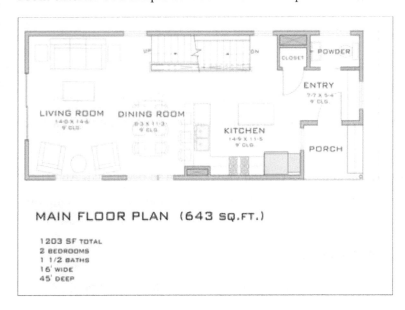

Main Level Layout of a Simple Barndominium

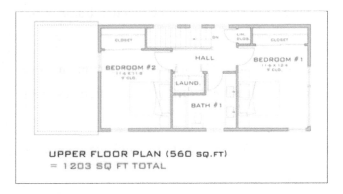

Upper Level Floor Plan of a Simple Barndominium

Would you prefer the layout of a simple barndominium even if you had less space? This small three-level, two-story plan may be built on nearly any urban lot.

The clever division of the living and sleeping areas makes this barndominium floor design unique. With the bedrooms located on the upper and foundation levels and the living area on the main floor, this design is easily adaptable to suit a variety of lifestyles.

A Modern Barndominium's Floor Plan

The exterior front of a modern barndominium layout plan

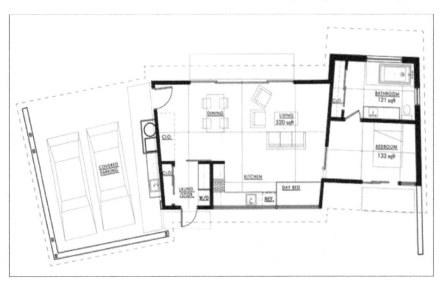

The main floor plan of a contemporary barndominium

This rustic barndominium floor plan looks like it would fit in well in a Western movie. Its open floor plan and sloping extended roof make it an excellent weekend vacation home since they keep you cool in the summertime heat. Although the outside is simple and unassuming, the interior will undoubtedly impress.

Little cottage bedrooms, get started! This layout provides lots of room for unwinding without feeling cramped, thanks to its roomy master bedroom suite and open living-dining area. With so many beautiful windows and sliding doors that open to the outside, this barndominium floor plan is perfect for anyone looking for a closer connection to nature.

Take a close look at this floor plan to choose which aspect we like best. After a gluttonous weekend, a well-placed daybed just off the kitchen is the perfect place to unwind.

The layout of a barndominium featuring a covered porch

A covered porch and front exterior of a barndominium floor plan

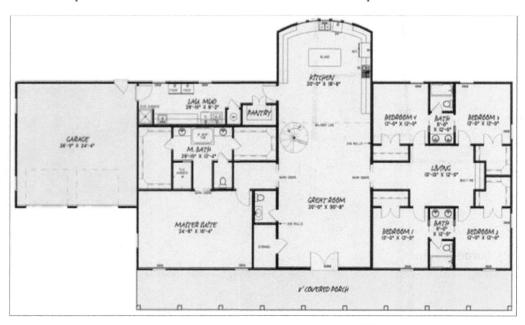

Main Level Floor Plan of a Covered Porch Barndominium

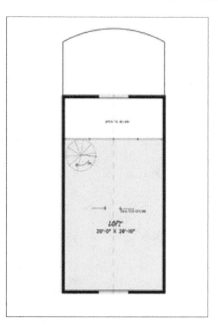

A barndominium's upper floor plan featuring a covered porch

Discover a barndominium floor plan that maximizes the use of a large property. 3,277 square feet in total. The 5,500-square-foot, 3.5-bathroom plan is perfect for someone who enjoys barndominium architecture but wants to up the ante. Thoughtful extras include a mudroom and an ensuite bathroom with two walk-in closets off the master bedroom.

The spacious great room offers plenty of space for lounging, entertaining, and dining. The four more adjoining bedrooms and separate living area in the middle provide more space and privacy for visitors or older kids.

There won't be a shortage of counter space in the kitchen, but you might be too busy admiring the scenery out that gorgeous bow window to spend much time cooking (which is why delivery is available).

Floor Plan for a Tiny Barndominium

The front outside floor plan of the tiny barndominium

The Tiny Barndominium Floor Plan's Main Level

A versatile addition to any backyard would be this compact floor plan shaped like a barn. Use it as a pool house, guest house, or bunkie for outdoor activities. With this one, the possibilities are truly endless.

Explain what a bunkie is. To read more from House Beautiful, click this link.

This adorable and practical floor plan offers plenty of utility in a compact 388 square feet. feet. With a large bedroom, a kitchenette, and two bathrooms featuring walk-in showers, this arrangement provides all the amenities need for a comfortable stay.

The layout of a barndominium featuring a workshop

Front exterior floor plan of a barndominium with workshop

The Barndominium's Main Floor Plan with the Workshop

This barndominium floor plan includes everything. Really not at all.

For any car enthusiast, this layout with two garages, an RV berth, and a workshop is perfect. Family members won't have to worry about hearing noise from the workshop area because the bedrooms, great room, and living room are located on the opposite end of the house. After a hard workday, cleaning up will be a breeze thanks to the mud room and adjoining laundry room, so feel free to be as careless as you wish.

Are you in need of some fresh air? Not a problem. This floor plan has two covered outdoor areas: one in the front and one at the back. Thanks to the gorgeous back patio that opens to an all-season lanai, you can enjoy the outside in any weather.

Layout of a Loft-Style Barndominium

Front exterior floor plan of a loft-equipped barndominium

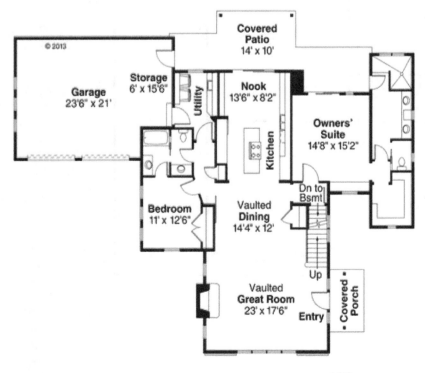

Main Level Layout for a Loft-Style Barndominium

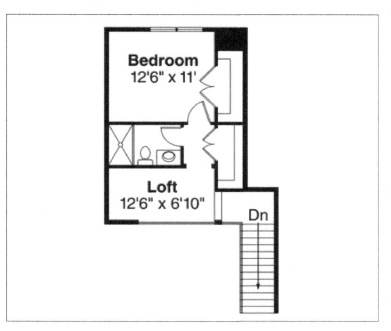

Loft-Style Upper Floor Plan for a Barndominium

This is an updated version of the classic barndominium facade.

The overall design welcomes natural light. With big barn doors opening out from the great room and soaring ceilings throughout the common rooms, this home makes the most of open space to make it seem and look much larger than it is.

The main suite's en suite bathroom features a huge L-shaped bathtub and an expansive walk-in closet. You are welcome to have a dance party in the morning while you take a shower. We won't divulge it.

A barndominium's floor plan featuring a garage apartment

Front exterior floor plan of a barndominium with a garage apartment

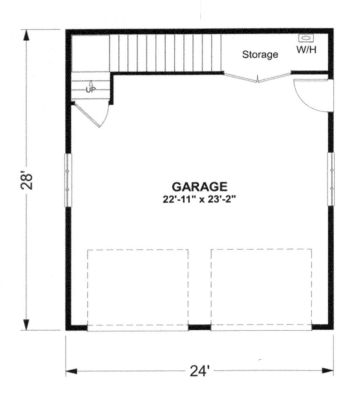

A Barndominium's Main Floor Plan with a Garage Apartment

Diagram of a Barndominium's upper floor featuring a garage apartment

This two-story floor plan for a barndominium is perfect for craftsmen and crafters and a great example of how to make the most of 562 sq. feet.

This design would make a fantastic first home if you or a family member is used to apartment living but desires more space for work and creativity. The main floor offers the perfect open space for a garage, workshop, or studio. Just above is the living area, complete with a kitchen, bedroom, banquette, and bathroom. Thanks to the enormous storage space throughout, you can leave behind the days of living in apartments with just one closet.

The Duplex Barndominium's layout

The front outside floor plan of the duplex barndominium

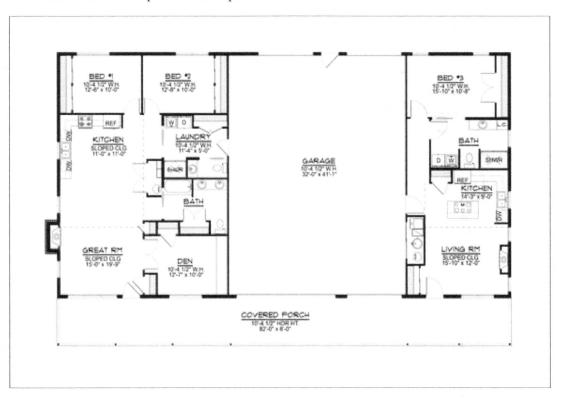

Duplex Barndominium Floor Plan: Main Floor Plan

One of the strangest barndominium floor plans we've seen so far is this one. This one-story design splits the house into two separate living zones by placing a carport in the center.

Featuring living and sleeping quarters on both sides, a kitchen, and a bathroom, this house is perfect for multigenerational households or for giving guests a little extra privacy. But worry not—you can stay in touch with your loved ones at all times thanks to the gorgeous covered porch that connects the two living areas.

An example of a barndominium floor plan with a courtyard

The front outside floor plan of a barndominium with a courtyard

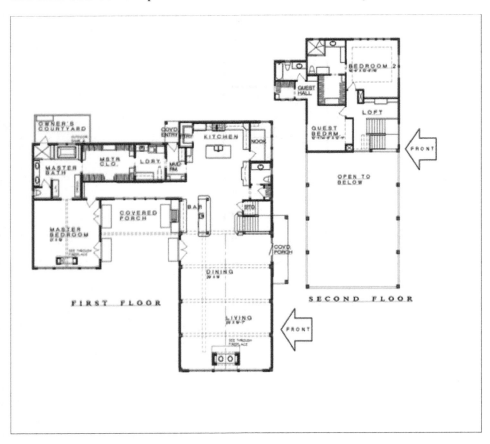

Plans for the Main and Upper Levels of a Barndominium with Courtyard

This lavish barndominium's floor plan is the stuff dreams are made of. With its two see-through fireplaces, floor to ceiling windows, owner's patio, and lofty vaulted ceilings, this home is one of the most luxurious on the list.

One of the most unique aspects of its design is the bar area. If you're someone who prefers a more casual dining experience, this well-positioned bar is a great place to host guests.

If your visitors decide to stay the night, that's acceptable. The loft directly upstairs houses two more bedroom suites. This multipurpose area might easily be utilized as a home office or as a private space for family members who need their own place.

Breezy Barndominium Floor Plan

Front Exterior Floor Plan of a breezy barndominium

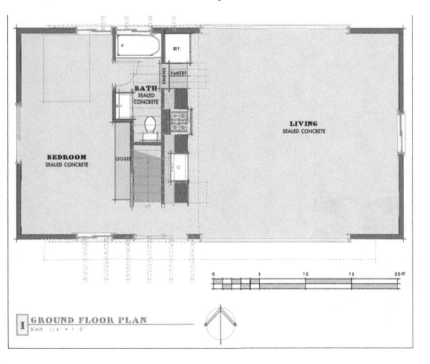

The Breezy Barndominium Floor Plan's Main Floor

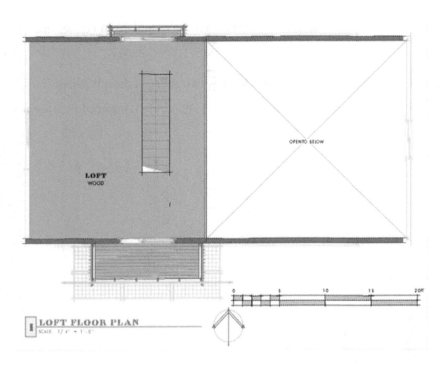

Breezy Barndominium Floor Plan: Upper Floor Plan

The homes on this list wouldn't be called barndominiums if they didn't resemble barns in some manner. But this one-bedroom arrangement is the finest floor plan to keep the barn vibe.

This floor plan may look barnlike, yet it offers a unique link to the outside world. Large barn doors on either side allow the entire living room of the house to open up to the outside. Cool summer breezes are certain to reach every corner of the house thanks to its clever design. On cool nights, use the balcony off the top loft.

A Barndominium's Floor Plan Featuring Outdoor Space

A barndominium's front exterior floor plan featuring an outside area

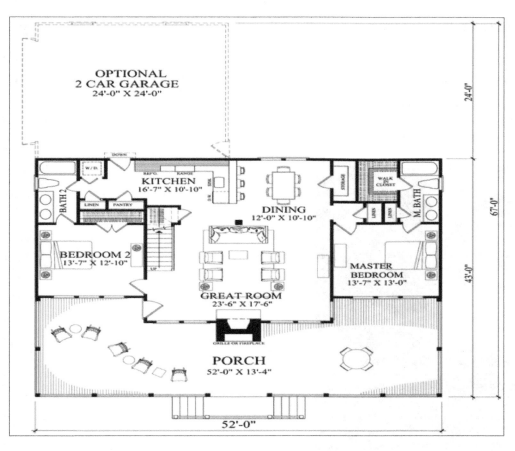

A Barndominium's Main Floor Plan Featuring Outdoor Space

A Barndominium's Upper Floor Plan Featuring Outdoor Space

This creative design takes the classic covered porch to a whole new level. With its central fireplace, this stylish outdoor space is a perfect way to extend the great room and stays warm on chilly evenings.

The goal of this floor plan was to create a gathering area in the middle of the house, with the main and guest suites on either side.

On the upper floor, there are two distinct bedrooms for guests or family members who need a bit additional seclusion. A cozy extended nook in one of the bedrooms would be perfect for a window seat or little reading nook.

Open Concept for a Barndominium Floor Plan

Front exterior of an open concept barndominium floor plan

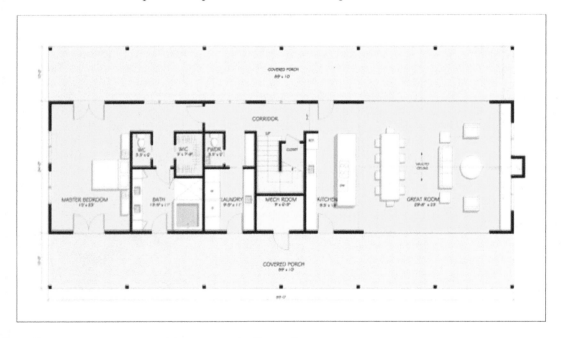

An open-concept barndominium's main floor plan

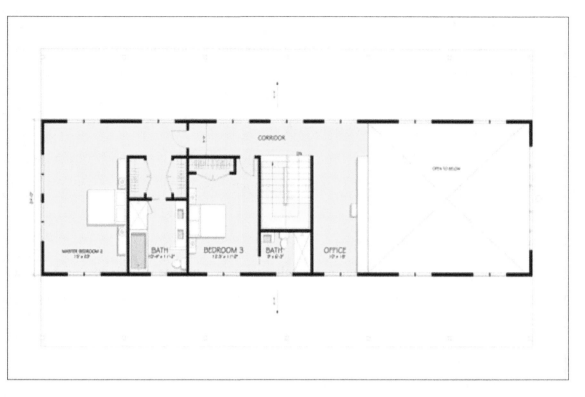

Upper Floor Plan of an Open Floor Plan for a Barndominium

In addition, the modern design of this two-story barndominium floor plan keeps everything organized, spotless, and simple to utilize.

The wide covered porches on both sides and the lofty ceilings in the main space are unquestionably the most noticeable features of this floor design. However, if you look a little closer, you'll realize that every part of this house was picked with care.

A summons from below. Every room on the main floor has easy access to the long porches, so you can take advantage of the chance to get some fresh air while heading to the kitchen or laundry room. The office area faces the expansive great room, so you never miss a "dinner's ready!" moment.

How many different kinds of basements can a barndominium have?

- The same types of basements seen in conventional houses can also be found in barndominiums, including: • Partially finished basements
- Basements with walk-outs
- Fully equipped basements

Concrete makes up the majority of basement walls, and it could also be used for the floors. The floor of a fully finished basement is the same size as the structure's frame. It occupies the same area as the basement and first floor.

Typical barndominium construction uses post frames or steel frames. The post columns have earth anchors in them. It may be necessary to fasten the posts to the frames above the crawl area if the basement is completely finished. Although there hasn't been much of a shift in the constructing process, it's still preferable to deal with a builder with prior experience.

A partially finished basement is a simple method to do this. Some basements are limited to the lowest level of the house. The remainder of the first floor is supported by a section of concrete. In a barndominium, building a half-basement is less expensive and simpler than building a complete one.

Because the concrete slab continues to support the house's perimeter, the frame is still being constructed in the same manner. You won't receive as much additional space, which is a drawback.

The most challenging option to construct is a walk-out basement, which is typically reserved for homes with hills or slopes. You can install a door because the back end is at ground level because to the sloping base. But because it is more difficult to operate, this option is more expensive.

Barndominiums do well in basements for the following reasons:

Including a bottom level in a barndominium has several advantages, including increasing the overall size of the area. Lower levels are frequently utilized for extra living space, cleaning, or storage. Additional square footage may be helpful if you need a modest floor plan and have a tiny land.

You are also safe in basements. Concrete walls offer greater security than a house's steel or wood framework. During inclement weather or storms, you can take refuge in the basement.

Due to its underground construction, basements typically have significantly lower temperatures than upper floors. In order to stay cool when building a barndominium in a hot climate, a basement can be useful.

Why Basements Are Not Suitable for Barndominiums

One of the biggest issues with constructing a basement below a barndominium is the cost. It takes labor, materials, and time to prepare the ground for the basement and pave the walls with concrete.

For a complete or partially finished basement, basement foundations cost roughly $33 per square foot. The average cost of a crawl space is $13 per square foot. A concrete slab is the least expensive option, costing about $7 per square foot.

A concrete slab can be made faster as well. Your wait time for a basic slab may be as little as a few days or as long as two weeks if the barndominium floor design is large enough. Several weeks could be needed to complete a basement.

Furthermore, keep in mind that an above-ground living space is not always a suitable substitute for a basement. Most of the time, basement rooms aren't considered bedrooms unless they have doors and windows that open to the outside. This is typically only feasible with a walk-out basement.

If you want to use the basement as an additional living space, there might not be as much natural light in the space. You may need to install enough artificial lighting and finish the walls, ceiling, and flooring in order to live in the area.

Alternatives to Basements for Barndominiums

If installing a basement foundation is not what you want to accomplish, you can install a crawl space or a block foundation.

Slab foundations, which have a simple, flat cement slab, are used to build most dwellings. They are simpler to manufacture, so you can get started on creating the barndominium's frame sooner. Slabs are also the least expensive option.

Generally speaking, crawl spaces are low, vacant rooms that are three to four feet high. Just enough room to crawl. The main purposes of crawl spaces are extra storage and access to the area underneath the floors.

Building a tunnel with a slab surrounding it to fit the barndominium structure is similar to building a partial basement. In this manner, the design of the frame can be left unchanged.

Final Thoughts on Barndominium Basements

Basements in barndominiums have their advantages and disadvantages. You will need to put in additional labor to finish your new home if you choose to add a basement. It is possible to postpone the deadline by a minimum of one month.

Adding a basement will further increase the expense of the project, particularly if you wish to finish it out or have a walk-out.

Although basements have certain drawbacks, they are nevertheless a valuable addition to any barndominium. They give you more space and allow you to set up your dryer and washer. If the basement is large enough, you can even complete the interior to create a game room or home theater.

In the end, barndominiums have many of the same design options as traditional homes. Any type of basement is possible, albeit it may require more steps and labor. It may be best to work with a builder who has experience with basement foundations if you wish to add a basement.

The best way to learn more about barndominiums and the concept of a basement-equipped barndominium is to get the Barndominium Life Program.

Chapter 7

Barndominium Garage Doors

A modern designer's ideal home was constructed with the help of aluminum garage doors.

Three sources of inspiration were light, barns, and ancient dogtrot houses. She ultimately acquired a stunning "Barndominium," a well-known new kind of house that blends contemporary and rustic architecture to create a large barn-like structure with an expansive breezeway that brings in plenty of natural light and links the inside to the outside. Kelly's barn is large enough for her active family of five, with room for a guest bedroom and a shop for her husband thanks to the Overhead DoorTM model 521. Situated on 15 acres of rural terrain in northern Louisiana, the barn is a working farm.

Garage doors are located on both ends of the breezeway, which runs through the center of the structure. The dwelling wing and the shop/office half of the space are divided by these doors. By opening a third garage door, it is simple to walk between the living room and the breezeway.

The living room and the house's encircling patio are separated by a fourth metal door. This brightens the area and allows Kelly's kids to ride their bikes and roller skates from the middle of the house to the outside. The family regularly hosts events, records live music, and conducts workshops in the open space.

The Door Above Glass and metal are combined in the Modern Metal Collection to create doors that are visually stunning, robust, and light-filled. Modern garage doors are a tool employed by designers to enhance and modernize creative spaces. The doors have a sleek appearance and inviting lines.

The Garage Door Claim

The sleek and modern glass garage doors leading into the living area of a "barndominium" are frequently one of the most sought-after design elements.

The Drawbacks of Garage Doors:

Let me start with the drawbacks: owning a garage door isn't always a bed of roses. For those considering purchasing a garage door, there are a few obvious drawbacks that they should be aware of.

1) Cost: A glass garage door is not something you can simply purchase like any other garage door. Not if you want to build houses according to the rules! Typically, there are two reasons why a residential garage door needs to be custom-made:

-R Value: This indicates how well a door blocks heat transfer, or insulates against it. It needs to be up to the "R Value" requirements for a house set by your building department. Depending on the zone, you'll require between R-13 and R-25 (non-ceiling). A higher R-Value is preferable. Apart from the features that a standard garage door (intended for an unconditioned area) offers, the additional insulation typically needs to be manufactured specifically, raising the expense.

—U-Value: This is a figure that indicates how much heat escapes through a window or piece of glass and how well it blocks heat. In technical terms, U-Value can be calculated by dividing the rate of heat transfer through a material (such as a window) by the temperature differential throughout the window's structure. Heat retention is more likely to occur in low-U values. Similar to R-Value, most garage doors aren't constructed in accordance with residential/conditioned space U-Value building codes. This necessitates custom manufacturing, which raises the price.

2) Sealing: You won't get a garage door that seals along the bottom like a sliding door or a door with tracks, no matter who promises you so. It isn't achievable. Our slab was graded to match the door opening, and we had seals fabricated to fit our floors and door precisely. Numerous different approaches have been attempted by other clients and residences in an attempt to obtain "the perfect seal," but to no avail.

What is meant by that? that a large hole in your wall allows a lot of air, rain, or insects to enter? Not at all! Even with a glass garage door, a home can be extremely energy-efficient. There might be a few more bugs visible (pill and rollie-pollies are the worst ones), but nothing really unsettling or disgusting. However, bear in mind that it will not close like a track-based door. The arrangement just forbids it.

3) Privacy: A glass garage door is used. This implies that anyone can look in and that covering it with drapes from Target is not an option. Although it's not a major concern if you're building in the country, it's still something to consider. Although you can tint the glass, doing so will alter its color and reduce the amount of light coming in, which may not be what you want.

The Advantages of Garage Doors

The exciting part is about to begin. Yes, it's extremely lovely to have a glass garage door in your living room. We've identified the following benefits:

1. Let the daylight in. The greatest approach to take in the view or let in natural light is through a wall of windows. You may enjoy the outside view and allow in more light and air with a glass garage door.
2. It's incredibly useful to have a garage door in your living area. It may seem absurd, but having one makes moving large furniture pieces a breeze!

3. We've rollerbladed inside the house from the patio, which is quite cool. We open the door to let in the fresh scent of summer rain. People may move from the front yard to the living room with ease during our celebrations. The "coolness" factor of having a glass garage door in your home is undeniable!

Ultimately, you should weigh the advantages and disadvantages of each design component for your house and select the one that most closely matches your style, budget, and way of life.

Garage Plans with Barndominium Style

These garage plans remind us of barndominium plans because of their gable roofs, barn-style entrances, and rustic exteriors. Inside, open floor layouts provide ample space for vehicles, gardening equipment, or anything else you may think of. Certain plans have living quarters as well, so friends and family can stay in these buildings. Check out these practical garage ideas designed in the barndominium style.

Garage blueprint in the style of a barn Garage Design 1070-120:

Garage Farmhouse-Style

Front Angle The primary floor plan is displayed in the garage plan 1070-120, which has a farmhouse design.

With over 1,000 square feet of open space on the left side of this flexible garage concept, there is more than enough room for two automobiles. The building's living area, which includes a kitchen with a center bar, a bedroom with plenty of storage space, and a complete bathroom, is accessible from the living room on the right.

Garage That amounts to 2,500 square feet in the garage (1070–121).

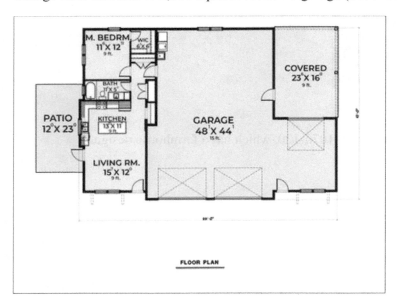

Outside the Front Garage Space: 2,500 square feet; Main Floor Plan: 1070-121

Without a doubt, this garage concept is larger than average. The structure offers an entire apartment and a ton of space for parking or working, making it ideal for both living and storage needs. A convenient apartment with a walk-in closet in the main bedroom, an open kitchen and living area, and a complete bathroom is located across the garage. The patio outside this apartment is also available for use by visitors.

Garage Plan in the Country Style

Front and Back of Country-Style Garage Plan 124-1052

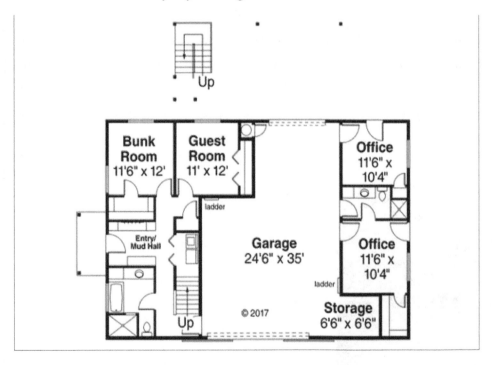

Main Floor Plan with a Country Style and Garage Plan 124-1052

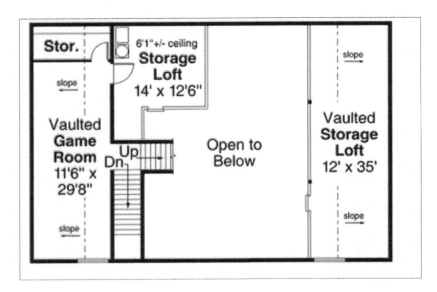

Upper Floor Plan for Garage Plan 124-1052 in a Country Style

This garage design has an exterior reminiscent of a traditional barn, complete with red siding, barn doors, and a dome topped with a wind vane. Inside are two distinct living areas on either side of a sizable parking lot. There's a full restroom in the center, and two offices adjacent to each other on the right. This enables you to operate a small business out of your house or allows multiple people to work from home. Surrounding the area are two bedrooms, a full bathroom, and a mud hall. People can remain there in comfort because of this. This is the second floor's vaulted game room/store area. Ascending to the highest level will lead you to an apartment featuring a gallery-style living and dining area, a bedroom suite, and even a covered terrace.

Adaptable Design for a Rural Garage

Front and rear views of Flexible Country Garage Plan 1064-75

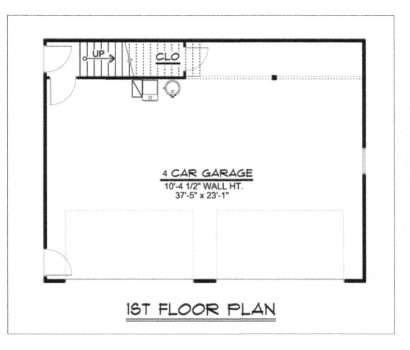

IST FLOOR PLAN

For Country Garage Plan 1064-75, the main floor plan

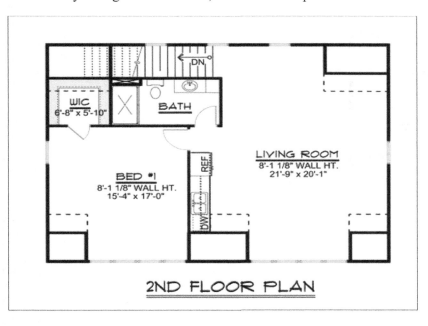

2ND FLOOR PLAN

There is an upper floor plan and flexibility in the 1064-75 country garage plan.

Up to four automobiles can fit on the main floor of this area, making it ideal for storing lawn equipment or recreational vehicles or family cars. There are stairs leading to the second floor, which features a spacious living area perfect for entertaining family and friends. There is a large walk-in closet in the bedroom with a bathroom close by. It is a terrific spot for people to stay, this lovely, snug addition.

Design a garage for a farmhouse.

Farmhouse Garage Plan 47-1090: Front and Back

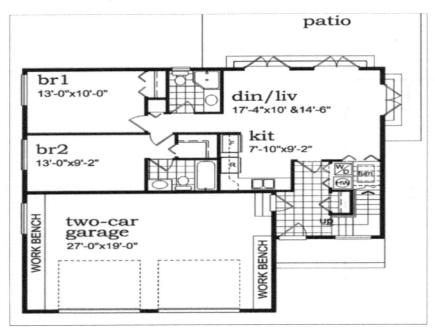

Farmhouse garage plan 47-1090: main floor layout

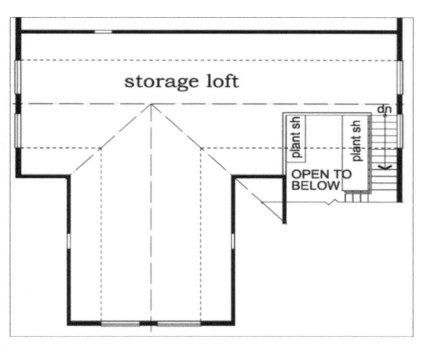

Inspired by a Farmhouse, Garage Plan 47-1090 - Upper Floor Plan

With a table on each side, this garage concept in the farmhouse style accommodates two automobiles in the front. The washing room and mudroom are conveniently located near by for quick access, and the connecting living and dining area at the back of the building is a terrific place to unwind. Visitors can stay alone on this floor because it has two beds and two bathrooms. A second-floor storage room could come in handy for keeping your belongings organized.

Plans for a Country Garage

Create a country garage plan. The Country Garage's facade 932-91 Plan 932-91 is a country garage plan.

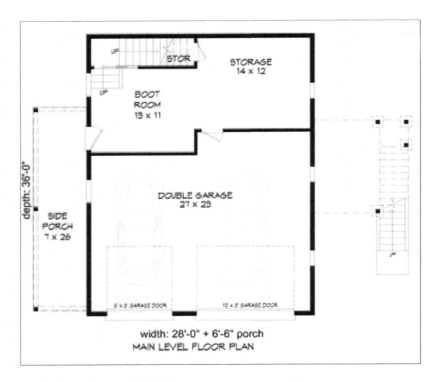

main floor layout 932-91 is a country garage plan.

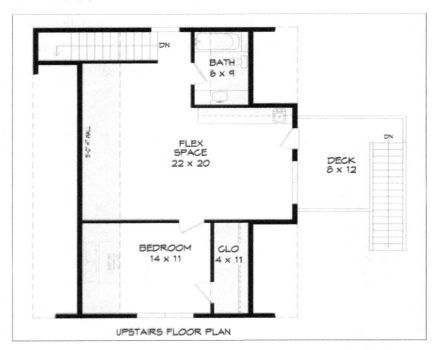

top floor layout

For those looking to maximize your living and storage space, this barndominium concept is ideal. There is a garage on the lower floor that has space for two automobiles. To keep the area tidy, there is a separate room in the back for storage and boots. A sizable atrium on the upper level leads to the second-floor deck. There is a bedroom with a spacious closet that surrounds this space. This garage plan is designed in the barndominium style, and the second level has a full bathroom that makes it an excellent guest apartment.

Plans for a rustic garage

Create a rustic garage plan. Design 117-483 is a rustic garage plan.

front and rear views The rustic garage plan 117-483's main floor plan

161

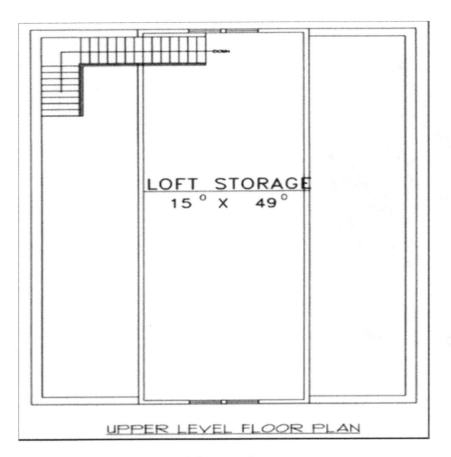

LOFT STORAGE
15^0 X 49^0

UPPER LEVEL FLOOR PLAN

Design 117-483 for a second-floor rustic garage

Require plenty of parking spaces? This unique plan's gambrel roof reminds me of traditional barn architecture. There's a heated car-sized shop area inside, and additional space for parking or store area is available on three sides. This main floor is ideal for you if you enjoy creating things because it offers plenty of workspace. This large loft area on the second story allows for convenient storage, making the most of every square foot in this rustic, barndominium-style garage layout.

Traditional Barn-Style Garage

A classic garage in the manner of a barn Conventional Garage in the Barn Style 124-1098

Front Angle The primary layout of the traditional barn-style garage (124-1098)

The upper floor plan of Garage in the Style of a Classic Barn, 124-1098

With almost 600 square feet of space on the upper floor, this building can serve as your home office, studio, or any other kind of space you require. It's convenient to take a break from conversations because there is a full restroom above.

What Distinguishes a Barndominium from a Pole Barn? Three Solid Arguments in Favor of Having Living and Storage Areas in the Same Building

Would you rather construct a barndominium or a pole barn? Utilize this comparison to determine the advantages and disadvantages of each option. Let's start by discussing what barndominiums are.

Pole barns and barndominiums are constructed using similar techniques. Actually, the original barndominiums were constructed on a horse ranch using abandoned barns. Pole framing, sometimes referred to as post-frame construction, has been used since the 1930s to swiftly construct stable houses and other agricultural structures. Horse barns are stable, which is one reason real estate developers decided to convert them into residences.

The first barndominiums were constructed in the 1980s. After a long time, people are increasingly choosing barndominiums over traditional homes. If you construct a barndominium, you might not need to construct a separate pole barn.

What Distinguishes a Barndominium from a Pole Barn?

A barndominium is a kind of dwelling that is constructed similarly to a pole barn. A pole barn is constructed with large posts buried down in the earth. Enough space is within for animals to be housed and fed thanks to the poles supporting the top and walls.

You can construct tall one-story buildings with the help of that pole frame. Most residences have ceilings that are 8 or 9 feet high, while most barns have ceilings that are 12 feet high. Within the upper portion of the barn, there might also be a loft or mezzanine area.

A pole barn's frame and a barndominium's frame are quite similar. However, before the frame is constructed, a base is poured. Many barndominium constructions are built on concrete slabs. The poles or posts are fastened to the base of the frame to increase its stability.

The primary distinction between a pole barn and a barndominium is the interior. Constructed to resemble a house, the barndominium features a living room, dining room, kitchen, bathrooms, and bedrooms.

Barndominium heating, electrical, and plumbing systems are identical to those in single-family homes. In the winter, a boiler heats the house, while a water heater prepares the water for usage. Unless animals or items need to be kept at a specific temperature, pole barns are typically not heated.

Reasons to Construct a Pole Barn

The main purpose of a pole barn is often to provide you with additional space. Common uses for a pole barn include:

- Housing animals
- Storing equipment and other items
- Hay storage
- Gatherings
- Garages
- Items to store
- Fun Things

If none of these reasons apply to your need for additional space, you could be better off constructing a barndominium. On the other hand, adding a building with a roof to your property at a low cost and with ease is possible with a pole barn.

A pole barn can be built quickly and affordably. If you employ a contractor, you should budget between $15,000 and $30,000 for a pole barn. DIY projects often cost $4000 or less. It normally costs $20 to $35 per square foot to build something. The frame alone may cost about $8 per square foot, but a wood-stud frame can run you about $10 per square foot.

The Case for Constructing a Barndominium

Building a pole barn is probably what you want to do if you require more space than a typical wood home can provide. A barndominium can provide you with the space you require and a place to live. Essentially, a barndominium is an oversized pole barn with an inside finish. However, there's a chance that some inside work is unfinished.

The open portion of the barndominium can be utilized in the same manner as a pole barn. The space can be utilized as a workshop, or it can be used to keep goods or pets.

You receive an attached barn, which offers several advantages.

- Easy to access
- Better cost control
- Using land more wisely

Constructing a house with an attached barn or work area is beneficial. Going outside from your house to the barn is not something you want to do. Depending on how the barndominium is configured, the living space and barn room may be connected by a door or hallway. You can utilize tools to create your own design, hire an expert to draft your blueprints, or look up floor plans online if you want to build a barndominium.

Additionally, building a barndominium is less expensive than building a pole barn and an independent house. One crew will undertake the necessary construction, saving you the expense of hiring two. It should save you money and time as compared to building each structure separately. Despite having two uses, a barndominium is less expensive to construct than a typical dwelling.

Another better use of your available space is a barn that is connected to your home. More area is needed to unite two separate buildings than to link them together as one. If you utilize less of your land now, you can always add more later. Knowing these concerns makes it much more important for you to budget for and secure insurance for your barndominium.

Is It Better to Build a Barndominium or a Pole Barn?

A pole barn is ideal for people who are content with their house and just need more space. It just takes a few days to erect a pole barn with the correct assistance.

If you want to improve the appearance of your living area while still needing storage space in a pole barn, building a barndominium can be a smart option. Constructing a barndominium is an affordable option for anyone who might require a new residence in the future. For example, you may live in an older house.

It is possible to construct a whole new home with a barn and living quarters. It's not necessary to construct two distinct buildings—you can just construct one. Constructing a new house and a barn simultaneously may need more time and money.

However, not everyone ought to construct a barndominium. It's likely that you'd prefer not to integrate your house and barn into one structure. For example, you can prevent noise from animals or a workplace by keeping the barn far from your home. People in the house might not be bothered by the noises coming from the barn.

Typically, pole barns are used as places to store goods or provide housing for animals. Although barndominiums are houses, they may contain spaces that could be utilized similarly to those of a pole barn.

If you currently own a home, adding a pole barn could help you expand your living space. If you'd like a new house with a pole barn, you may construct a barndominium.

Chapter 8

How To Budget For Building A Barndominium

Following that, we'll help you create a budget and estimate costs for building, site preparation, and interior finishing. Investigate funding options and ways to reduce costs for construction projects. By the time this book ends, you will be ready to begin your barndominium journey!

Understanding What Apartments Are

A barndominium is a type of residential building that combines living quarters with a workshop or barn. This odd arrangement of spaces has grown in popularity recently, particularly in rural locations, due to its affordability, versatility, and longevity.

An notion and an explanation

The phrase "barndominium" is derived from the words "barn" and "condominium," but it doesn't only relate to the arrangement of barn characteristics; other practical areas like garages, workshops, or even offices can be included.

Barndominium designs typically include high ceilings, an open floor layout, and large windows that let in lots of natural light. Metal is a common material for the outside since it resists weather and needs little maintenance. Any style can be used to adorn the interior, ranging from a sleek modern industrial look to a traditional rustic look.

In place of typical stick-built homes, barndominiums offer a unique experience for those looking for something different or in need of a separate space for business or hobbies.

Affordable barndominium at a reasonable price range.

Benefits of Building a Barndominium

There are several benefits to building a barndominium, some of which are listed below:

1. **Cost-Effectiveness:** Building a barndominium is sometimes less expensive than building a normal dwelling because it can be completed more quickly and with less materials. Metal has the potential to drastically reduce maintenance costs due to its resistance to rot, rust, and insect infestation.

2. **Energy Efficiency:** Metal buildings have great insulation properties that help lower the energy required for heating and cooling. A lot of barndominium owners also choose to include energy-efficient features, such solar panels or geothermal heating systems, in order to reduce their utility costs and their environmental effect.

3. **Durability:** A well-constructed barndominium may withstand harsh weather conditions and last longer than some typical stick-built dwellings. Furthermore, metal construction offers the best protection against fires, mildew, and insects.

4. **Customizability:** Using a barndominium as a blank canvas, homeowners can design the kind of life they want. When it comes to adding porches or lofts, or changing the way the rooms are arranged, the options are nearly endless.

5. **Multi-Functional Spaces:** Combining residential and functional facilities, like a workshop or barn, allows a property to be used in more creative ways. Homeowners can profit from the financial benefits of not having to rent additional workplace or storage, as well as the convenience of having these areas connected to their home.

Use Cases and Examples of Barndominiums

To accommodate a wide range of needs and preferences, barndominiums come in a number of sizes and shapes. Several applications for barndominium include:

1. Hobby Farms: Barndominiums are especially popular with hobby farmers because they provide them with the necessary combination of living space and practical places for their agricultural operations. Although the living spaces are cozy and practical, livestock, feed, and equipment can be kept in the attached barn.

2. Workshops or Garages: For those who need a sizable workshop space for businesses or hobbies, a barndominium design may be beneficial. Car owners, woodworkers, and even small-scale manufacturers may find that having a large, dedicated area connected to their home is more cost-effective and efficient.

3. Multi-Generational Living: Barndominiums can provide lodgings for families who wish to live in a multi-generational setting. It is possible to build separate living quarters for elderly family members so they can remain independent and alone, yet still be close to their loved ones.

4. Vacation Homes: Some people build barndominium vacation homes, usually in remote or rural locations where they can go fishing, shooting, and off-roading. These homes not only provide comfortable living quarters but also include space for storing tools and recreational vehicles.

5. Commercial ventures: Barndominiums can also be used as event venues, B&Bs, or commercial businesses like art studios or galleries. The unique and flexible space may be configured to accommodate multiple businesses and attract customers looking for something special.

How to Arrange Your Apartment

A barndominium is a type of hybrid residential and commercial structure that incorporates elements of both a barn and a condominium. Originally designed for agricultural use, they have evolved into flexible, multipurpose spaces that accommodate living and working requirements. Building and creating a barndominium requires careful planning even though it could be exciting. This guide will help you from start to finish in designing and building your perfect barndominium.

Determining Your Goals and Mission

Before you begin planning, you must decide what your barndominium is supposed to be used for. This will outline the necessary design factors and help you make informed decisions during the planning stage. To assist you in determining the goal of a barndominium, consider the following inquiries:

1. Which use—residential or commercial—will the space be put to? or both?
2. Is it large enough for a home office, workshop, or farmers' equipment storage?
3. What activities or events are scheduled in the region?
4. What specific needs or desires do the people living in the neighborhood have? How many people are going to live there?
5. When aging in place, are there any requirements for accessibility or adaptation?
6. Will the space be utilized for entertaining guests or organizing events?

Your comprehension of your purpose and goals will inform your decisions on the site, layout, materials, finishes, and any legal or regulatory requirements.

Selecting a Proper Location

The planning of your barndominium must include selecting the perfect location. This could be an existing parcel of land that you own or one that you wish to purchase. Keep the following considerations in mind when choosing the perfect spot:

1. Land size: Make sure the plot has enough room for your desired barndominium size and type, as well as for parking, storage, landscaping, and any other outside features.
2. Topography: Uneven or sloping ground can require additional engineering and raise construction costs. Consider how the structure will fit in with the surroundings.
3. Access to utilities: Determine whether gas, water, sewage, and electricity connections are present and easily accessible.
4. transfer and access: Ensure that the plot has convenient access to main routes, especially for the transfer of equipment or goods by businesses.

How to Lay Out Your Barndominium

Once the location and objective have been determined, begin designing the actual layout of your barndominium, taking functionality, flow, and aesthetics into consideration. You have three options: work with an architect, select one of the floor plans, or have BarndoPlans.com change an existing floor plan. Crucial elements of design to consider are:

1. the number and dimensions of residential structures' living rooms, bedrooms, and bathrooms.

2. The dimensions of commercial or multifunctional areas such as workshops, storage rooms, and garages.

3. Partition of space: How will the business and residential areas coexist? One room versus several rooms.

4. windows and doors arranged to take full advantage of the light, airflow, and views.

5. possibility of expansion or adaptable designs for future need.

Choosing Interior and Exterior Finishes

Your choice of finishes will significantly affect the overall appearance and feel of your barndominium. In light of the objective, lifestyle, and personal preferences, consider the following:

1. External materials: Brick, stone, or wood siding are substitutes for the standard metal or steel panels.

2. Roofing: To ensure durability and enough storm protection, choose from a variety of materials, colors, and styles.

3. Flooring: Select practical, low-care materials such as concrete, luxury vinyl, or tile.

4. Select the materials and style for the countertops, cabinets, and built-in storage in the kitchen and bathroom.

5. Electrical and lighting: Based on your needs, both practically and aesthetically, select outlets and lighting fixtures.

6. Insulation and energy efficiency: Create an appropriate insulation system to maintain comfort and reduce utility costs.

Understanding Regional Construction Standards and Codes

Lastly, educate yourself on the local building codes, zoning laws, and permissions that apply to the construction of barndominiums. Although some jurisdictions may have restrictions on how land is used, how big buildings may be, setbacks, and other aspects of your design, bear these considerations in mind when designing. Respecting established conventions and protocols can ensure a smooth construction process and reduce any legal issues.

Seek assistance from a local architect, builder, or compliance officer to manage these limits. Maintain positive relationships with your neighbors and the neighborhood to ensure a smooth transition during and after construction.

Planning a barndominium requires careful budgeting and cost estimation because constructing a new house or beginning a significant restoration project can be costly. However, you may create the perfect area that suits your unique requirements and tastes with the correct preparation, investigation, and careful thought. This book will cover all the many aspects of estimating building expenses, such as site preparation and land development charges, utility installation and connection fees, interior finishing prices, and accounting for additional costs and contingencies.

Making a Spending Plan and Projecting Costs

How to Estimate Building Expenses

To get a precise cost estimate for constructing your new home, consider the following factors:

Materials: Structure, Insulation, Siding, and Roofing

A significant portion of your budget will go toward purchasing materials for the foundation, frame, insulation, roofing, and siding, among other structural components of your house. Material costs can be greatly impacted by a number of factors, including the size and kind of construction (steel or wood frame, for example), the materials used, and local rates.

Be prepared to look into suppliers and contractors in order to get an accurate quote for these necessary construction materials.

Labor and Expert Service Costs

The cost of labor and professional services will also be factored into your building budget. The intricacy of the job, local labor costs, and their degree of skill can all affect their costs. Designers, architects, general contractors, and subcontractors—which comprise individuals or groups with specialized knowledge in certain building tasks, such electrical, plumbing, and framing—are all subject to these costs. It is best to budget for the licenses, examinations, and compliance certificates that the local building authority want.

Costs for Site Development and Land Development Included

The costs associated with site work and land development charges include the costs of grading, excavation, and site preparation. These expenses can up quickly, particularly in areas with unfavorable soil or steep inclines. There may also be costs associated with building a driveway, sidewalk, or retaining wall. It is imperative to include in any expenses related to stormwater management, erosion prevention, and environmental conservation that may be required by local ordinances.

Keeping Track of Utility Connection and Installation Fees

At a new construction site, utility lines for power, water, sewage, and natural gas may need to be erected or extended. These rates can vary greatly depending on your region, the utility company's requirements, and local legislation. In addition to installation costs, ongoing utility connection and service fees may have an impact on the project budget.

Accounting for Interior Finishing Expenses

Drywall, Paint, Textures, and Flooring

All materials, including drywall, paint, and flooring, as well as any special treatments or finishes, are included in the cost of interior finishing. The intended style and feel will determine how much these materials cost; custom or high-end materials can drive up costs significantly, while basic paint and flooring options are more reasonably priced.

Plumbing, electrical, and HVAC systems

Complete HVAC (heating, ventilation, and air conditioning) system installation and setup are additional expenses that can make your budget more difficult to manage. The appliances and fixtures chosen, the quality of the materials, and the necessary level of energy efficiency can all have a significant impact on these costs.

Considering Additional Expenses and Backup Plans

Your building budget should include for any additions, such as outside kitchens, pools, or landscaping, as well as any changes to the lighting, cabinetry, or appliances. Window coverings, furniture, and other finishing touches should all be factored into the budget.

Lastly, always have backup plans ready. The project's budget and schedule may be impacted by unforeseen circumstances like weather fluctuations or supply chain interruptions. To ensure you have adequate cash on hand to handle unforeseen expenses, as a general rule of thumb, you should budget for a contingency reserve equivalent to 10-15% of the anticipated cost.

How to Raise Money for Your Barndominium Project

The financing of a barndominium project must be thoroughly planned, investigated, and comprehended in terms of the various financial options. It's crucial to look into multiple funding sources and to prepare your loan application and accompanying documents with attention. This book will provide you with information on financing options, interest rate considerations, negotiation strategies, and documents to assist you secure the best financing terms for your barndominium project.

Analyzing the Financing Options

A variety of finance options, including home equity lines of credit (HELOCs), construction loans, mortgages, and personal loans, should be considered when financing a barndominium project. There may be more financing choices accessible.

Mortgages and construction loans

A conventional mortgage or a construction loan can be excellent options for financing your barndominium project. The cost of labor, building materials, and site acquisition is typically covered by a mortgage. A construction loan, which may be converted into a regular mortgage once the project is completed, may be used to fund the actual construction of the barndominium.

Construction loans frequently need a bigger down payment percentage of the expected total loan value and have higher interest rates than mortgages. Nonetheless, they do offer lenient conditions and finance accessibility during the construction stage.

You must look at a number of lenders and loan packages in order to choose the finest mortgage or construction financing for your barndominium project.

Home equity credit lines (HELOCs)

A handy way to finance your barndominium project could be with home equity lines of credit (HELOCs), if you currently own your home or a significant portion of the equity in it and you haven't sold it yet. You may borrow money against the value of your home with this type of loan, sometimes at a lower interest rate than you would pay on a traditional mortgage or construction loan. It's possible that deducting interest from a home equity loan will result in tax savings.

HELOCs usually have two components: a draw term, during which you can access cash as needed, and a repayment duration. Keep in mind that the value of your home will decide the maximum amount you can borrow. You can also discuss the specific terms and conditions of a home equity loan (HELOC) with your lender.

Personal Loans and Other Alternative Sources of Funding

A personal loan is an additional option for financing a barndominium project, especially if you have a stable income stream and solid credit history. The fixed interest rates and repayment plans that these loans frequently provide could be helpful for budgeting.

Conversely, personal loans, as opposed to mortgages or home equity lines of credit (HELOC), may have higher interest rates and smaller lending limits. They might therefore be more appropriate as a supplementary finance source or for smaller barndominium projects.

Crowdsourcing, loans from friends and family, and government subsidies and incentives for environmentally or energy-efficiently built structures are among more non-traditional funding sources.

Getting Ready for Loan Applications and Documentation

After determining the best type of loan and researching your financing options, it's time to prepare your loan application and any necessary supporting documentation. Prepare any necessary financial data, such as proof of income, outstanding debts, and assets. You might also need to submit specifics like building contracts or architectural drawings related to the barndominium project.

Ensure that all necessary documentation is gathered, accurate, up to date, and organized. Talk to the lender of your choosing about the requirements for your application, and be prepared to provide any additional information or supporting evidence they may request.

Haggling over interest rates and loan terms

To ensure long-term financial stability and control costs, it's critical to bargain for the best loan terms and interest rates when financing your barndominium project. Before you start bargaining, do some research on current market interest rates and familiarize yourself with the products that other lenders are offering.

Your credit history, down payment size, and overall financial status will all have a significant impact on your qualifying for a certain interest rate. Aim for the lowest rates while considering the terms of the loan, such as the length of the repayment term and any early penalties.

Never be afraid to speak with other lenders to compare deals or request better conditions on a loan. Speaking with a mortgage broker or financial advisor could also be beneficial in helping you negotiate the best financing terms for your barndominium project.

Tips for Maintaining Your Budget While Building

Working Together with Trusted Professionals

One of the most important tips for keeping within your building budget is to work with trustworthy professionals. Working with a reliable general contractor, architect, and other subcontractors is required for this. When selecting a professional for your task, it is imperative that you get many bids and assess each candidate's expertise, credentials, and references. Additionally, be sure they have the necessary insurance and licenses for the specific work at hand.

The success of your building project will ultimately depend on the qualified employees you choose. Successful teams with experience can provide a reliable estimate and collaborate well to manage costs and avoid delays in the project timeline. Because of this, investing time in team selection and research is necessary to provide a more efficient and cost-effective building process.

Regularly tracking expenses and progress

It is essential to closely monitor spending and progress in order to preserve financial stability while developing. This calls for frequent site inspections and comprehensive progress reports that take into consideration all project-related costs, such as labor and supplies. Being actively involved will enable you to make the required changes to the building design, reducing financial risk and helping you stay within your budget.

It's also crucial to set up a system for keeping track of expenditures and contrasting them with the initial budget. This means planning for regular budget reviews, which depending on the complexity and duration of the project, may be done once a week or once a month. These evaluations can help you identify any patterns or discrepancies in your spending that might need to be addressed to maintain your financial goals on course.

Maintaining Effective Communication with Contractors

Good communication is essential to construction budget management. Maintaining communication with your contractors and subcontractors is necessary to ensure that everyone is aware of the project's financial constraints, expectations, and deadlines. Regular meetings or conference calls should be scheduled to discuss project updates and address any problems. Encourage frank and transparent communication amongst team members.

Additionally, having clear contractual agreements that outline the tasks to be completed, the deadlines for payments, and the procedure for handling change orders will help avoid misunderstandings and arguments and save you time and money when it comes to resolving disputes. Open channels of communication and a solid corporate culture will help you better manage changes and prevent potential overspending.

Methods of Value Creation and Cost-Reduction

Techniques for cost-cutting and value engineering are helpful instruments for managing building budgets. Finding areas where costs can be reduced without sacrificing the project's functioning or final quality is known as value engineering. This can mean utilizing prefabricated components, searching for alternatives to resources, and accelerating the construction process.

Another strategy is to negotiate lower material costs through bulk purchasing and volume discounts. Make sure you carefully consider the financial implications of each design element, and be prepared to determine which ones can be modified in order to stay within your allocated budget.

Acclimating to Unexpected Setbacks and Postponements

Any construction project will frequently run into unanticipated problems and delays, so staying within budget requires being adaptive and flexible. This means anticipating potential issues and developing contingency plans to address them. These challenges include unforeseen conditions at the site, a shortage of personnel, issues obtaining permits, or delays in the supply of materials.

It's imperative to react quickly to unanticipated disruptions and adjust project goals as necessary. This might mean reviewing the budget once more and allocating money to deal with new issues. By handling unforeseen issues early on, you can reduce their impact on the cost and timeline of your project and ultimately ensure a successful and cost-effective building process.

What factors should be considered when budgeting for a barndominium?

When creating a barndominium budget, consider items such as the price of the property, the building materials, the permits, the style, and the design. Costs for labor, utilities, exterior and interior finishes, and any additional customizations should not be overlooked.

What is the total cost to build a barndominium?

To determine the total cost, estimate the price per square foot while accounting for building and customization expenses. Next, calculate the square footage of the perfect barndominium. Finally, multiply the price per square foot by the total square footage.

Is it feasible to reduce the cost of building a barndominium?

Using energy-efficient materials, choosing a simpler design, buying a prefabricated building kit, or considering doing some of the work yourself can all help reduce costs. To find the best deal, compare prices and obtain quotes from multiple contractors.

What factors influence the price per square foot of a barndominium?

The cost per square foot is affected by a number of factors, including the complexity of the floor plans, the type of foundation, local labor costs, and special features like fixtures and finishes. Additional upgrades like insulation and energy-efficient windows also play a part.

How do construction loans and other financing options work when starting a barndominium?

Construction loans are short-term loans used to fund the building process. They usually convert to a longer-term mortgage with higher interest rates once construction is completed. Applying for a construction loan requires having a clean credit history, complete building plans, and accurate estimates.

Which permits and rules do I need to consider while budgeting for my barndominium?

Depending on where you live, different permissions and expenses can be required. Local zoning, building, and environmental regulations have a big impact on permit costs. To find out the requirements and associated costs, contact the local government authorities.

Made in the USA
Monee, IL
02 June 2024

59251782R10103